TradingView Pine Script Progr
Second Edition on VERSION 5 of PINESCRIPT
Copyright ©2021 by Achal

Trademarks
Pine Script is a TradingView platform-specific language for coding technical indicators and strategies. The use of a term in this book should not be regarded as affecting the validity of any trademark or service mark.

Warning and Disclaimer
Every effort has been made to make this book as complete and accurate as possible, but no warranty or fitness is implied. The information provided is on an "as is" basis. The author and the publisher shall have neither liability nor responsibility to any person or entity with respect to any loss or damages arising from the information contained in this book.

About the Author

Achal has more than 20 years of experience in computer programming as a hobbyist. He has a Bachelor's degree in Mechanical Engineering and a Master's degree in Management from the premier B school of India. The author has about 15 years of experience in International Trading. He is also an Author of the Udemy online video course **"Creating Trade Strategies & Backtesting using PineScript"**. He is currently working for a renowned Trading Company in India. His broad interest includes Stock and Commodity Market Research.

You can reach Achal by emailing him at **achalmeena@gmail.com**

Tell Us What You Think!

It is intended for programmers with a basic understanding of programming or those with no prior experience. As the reader of this book, you are our most important critic and commentator. If there are any improvements we can make to make this better, or if there are any areas you'd like us to add to future editions, we'd love to hear from you. If you have any suggestions, we would appreciate hearing from you.

Email: achalmeena@gmail.com

Dedicated to my Lovely Daughter Ammie

Table of content

Introduction

Welcome to the second edition of "TradingView Pine Script Programming From Scratch," updated for version 5 of PineScript. Based on the success of my earlier books, video course on Udemy, and feedback from the readers, I have written every single chapter of the book to make it more suitable for beginners like you who want to get started with scripting in PineScript for developing custom indicators, backtesting, and executing strategies in the TradingView Platform. Most of the material in this book has been taken from my earlier two books and updated appropriately for the latest version 5 of PineScript. The new edition has also allowed me to improve this book and add a few more topics for more comprehensive coverage.

Of course, it's a straightforward book to read and understand the concepts and programming skills introduced in the book. However, the good part is that this book offers many sample programs and exercises with clear explanations and answers, which make the concepts of PineScript easier to understand.

"TradingView Pine Script Programming From Scratch" provides a good starting point for you in PineScript programming. It covers essential topics in PineScript and lays a solid foundation for a beginner like you. After reading this book, you'll be able to write basic PineScript programs on your own to develop indicators.

You will benefit from reading this book and applying the programming skills gained to real problems. You could take full advantage of the TradingView Platform by understanding the concepts and logic behind the trade scripts of other Pine programmers. PineScript programming would also enable you to bypass restrictions imposed by the TradingView platform on the number of indicators that a user with a free subscription can use.

Who Should Read This Book?

If this is your first time learning any programming language, this book is written for you. In this book, I assume that the readers have no prior programming experience. If you have some knowledge of computers and working experience in Excel, that would be great.

Programming Examples

As mentioned before, this book includes numerous useful programming examples with explanations. These examples will guide you in utilizing various data types and functions available in PineScript.

Each example presents a listing of the PineScript program, followed by the generated output. The example also provides an analysis of how the program functions. Special icons are utilized to highlight each part of the example: INPUT, OUTPUT, and ANALYSIS

In the example presented in Listing IN.1, the input you provide is located under the Input icon, and the program's resulting output from Listing IN.1 is displayed under Output. Below the output, you will find a comprehensive program analysis under the Analysis icon.

INPUT LISTING IN.0.1 Plot value of close on chart

The code below is the default code generated by the TradingView platform when you click on "New Blank Indicator" in the PineScript editor.

```
1: // This source code is subject to the terms of the Mozilla Public License 2.0
2: // © Creating Trade Strategies & Backtesting using PineScript - Udemy
3:
4: //@version=5
5: indicator("My Script")
6: plot(close)
```

Unlike other programming languages that are executed once to obtain a result, Pine Script is executed every time a new bar is formed. This unique feature of multiple script executions sets it apart from other programming languages.

The execution of the script for each bar, triggered by the formation of a new bar, can pose challenges for traditional programmers in grasping the concept.

OUTPUT LISTING IN.0.1

Below is the output chart generated by the input provided in the above box. This code is for plotting the close values on the chart.

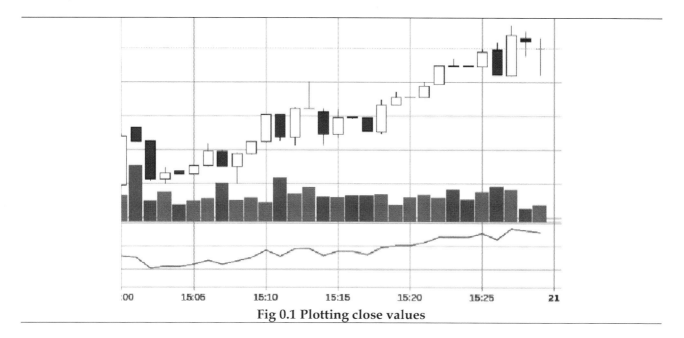

Fig 0.1 Plotting close values

The close value is plotted below the existing chart.

ANALYSIS LISTING IN.0.1

Comments are used in code to make it easier for programmers to understand when it's read by other programmers. Anything written as a comment is not considered part of the code and is ignored by the TradingView platform during execution. In PineScript, we have libraries and code contributed by other coders like yourself. You can download and use these codes for your own purposes. However, to understand what a specific code does, you may need to read the instructions or information provided as comments by the code's developers.

Lines 1 and 2 in the code are commented out and not included in the program's code. Comments are indicated by two consecutive slashes ('//'). You can write anything under a comment, such as copyright information or instructions for other programmers to understand the code. A comment can occupy an entire line, as shown in Lines 1 and 2, or it can start after the code on the same line, as demonstrated in Line 6 in the example below:

```
5: indicator("My Script")
6: plot(close) //code to plot close values
```

The third line is left blank, and the comment symbol is placed on the line following it. However, line 4 serves as a special instruction to the TradingView platform, indicating the intended version of PineScript. Line 4 cannot be considered a commented line. If you don't specify the script version, the TradingView platform will automatically assume it to be the latest version.

At the time of writing this book, the latest version of PineScript is version 5. There are differences between older versions of PineScript and the current version. You may encounter issues when executing scripts written in older versions without specifying the script version.

Line 5 contains the name of the script, which in this case is "My script." Line 6 provides an instruction to draw the closing price on the screen. Chapter 2 delves into a detailed analysis with a complete example.

Summary and Workshop

Each chapter ends with a "Summary" section followed by a workshop consisting of quiz questions and programming exercises. Appendix A to this book provides answers to these questions and sample solutions to the problems. To help you enhance your understanding of each lesson, you should try to attempt the questions and exercises provided.

Now, you're ready to start the journey of learning PineScript. Have fun reading this book, and enjoy programming in PineScript!

Chapter -1: Taking the First Step

Welcome to **Creating Trade Strategies & Backtesting using PineScript, Second Edition updated for version 5**. In this lesson, following topics have been covered:

- What is PineScript?
- Why you need to learn PineScript
- Assumptions About You
- Setting up your System

What is PineScript?

TradingView is an online platform that provides charting tools and various resources to its users. It has developed a scripting language called PineScript, which enables users to create custom indicators and trade strategies directly through their browser. PineScript is specifically designed for developing indicators and strategies within the TradingView environment and cannot be used on other websites, software, or applications. Unlike other programming languages, in PineScript, the code is executed each time a bar is formed, making it distinct in this aspect. Consequently, traditional programmers may encounter some challenges in comprehending how the script operates.

TradingView offers cloud-based storage, allowing users to store their scripts in the cloud without the need for local storage on their computers. However, it's important to note that if you have a proprietary algorithm or confidential trading strategy developed using PineScript, the code is hosted on TradingView's servers, over which you have no control.

Each PineScript code execution utilizes resources from TradingView's server or cloud. To ensure fair resource sharing among all users, TradingView has implemented certain limitations for free subscribers. If a user's code consumes excessive resources, TradingView may restrict the execution of that script on their servers. These limitations, imposed by the creators of PineScript, help maintain the platform's smooth operation and prevent any negative impact resulting from scripts that may disproportionately consume resources. The limitations mainly focus on factors such as the number of symbols added by a single program, long loops that increase execution time, memory usage, and script size.

PineScript, like any other modern programming language, has the following three features:

• **Readability**: Programs are easy to read. Syntax (rules for writing codes) of pinescript is similar to higher-level programming languages like python, java, or C.
• **Maintainability**: Cloud storage makes it easy to maintain programs.
• **Portability**: There is no restriction on the operating systems that can run programs created in browsers. Programs run on the server side of TradingView and are therefore easily ported to different computer platforms.

Every programming language requires a compiler or interpreter to translate the instructions written in that language into machine language that a computer can understand and execute. Different computers with varying machine architectures or operating systems may necessitate different compilers or interpreters for the same programming language. For example, in Windows, I use the Borland C compiler to compile C programs, while in Linux, a UNIX-based operating system, I need the GCC compiler. Programs compiled for one type of machine or operating system cannot be executed or used on other systems. This compilation issue renders such programs non-portable across different machines and operating systems. However, in the case of PineScript, the compiler or interpreter is located on the server side. In PineScript, users can input instructions from any platform, such as Linux, Mac, or Windows, using a web browser. The web browser converts the instructions into machine language and executes them on the server side, displaying the result.

In addition to the above, PineScript offers other advantages. Users can share their PineScript programs with others, allowing for community access. You can publish your PineScript programs and also utilize published scripts by other traders and users. This means you can incorporate parts of other users' code into your own program without having to code everything from scratch.

PineScript is a relatively concise programming language, which simplifies the coding process. You don't need to memorize numerous keywords or commands before starting to write programs in PineScript for creating indicators or strategies. The coding style, including the commands and syntax of PineScript, is quite similar to other high-level languages like Python, C, or Java. If you are familiar with any of these programming languages, learning PineScript will be a breeze.

Why do you need to learn PineScript?

I was initially drawn to TradingView because of its tools that allow users to create visually appealing and practical charts. Some other websites also utilize TradingView's interactive charts through a plugin on their own sites. TradingView stands out as one of the few platforms that offer stock data for multiple exchanges in smaller time frames. With a free account on TradingView, you can access three-minute timeframe data for the past 60 days.

Another aspect of TradingView that I appreciate is its nearly real-time data feed. Although there is a slight delay of around 2-3 seconds, it is much faster compared to other websites where the delay can exceed 15 seconds. I am satisfied with the charting and backtesting capabilities provided by this platform.

TradingView offers a free platform for creating indicators and trading strategies, whereas other similar platforms often charge a fee. This makes TradingView the preferred choice for both learners and traders to backtest their strategies (Achal, 2020).

Assumptions About Readers

This book is designed to teach you PineScript even if you have no prior programming experience, although some basic computer knowledge is beneficial. The pace at which you progress through the chapters is entirely up to you. By completing all the exercises provided in the book, you will become proficient and comfortable with the syntax (rules of writing code) and features of PineScript. Furthermore, you will gain experience in various tasks involved in PineScript programming. As you continue your learning journey, you will discover that there is always more to explore, not only about PineScript and how to maximize its potential but also about programming concepts in general. With dedication and ample practice, you can enhance your learning skills and make significant progress.

Setting Up Your System

All you need is a computer and an internet connection to compile and run your PineScript code from this book. I recommend a laptop or desktop computer due to their large screen size; however, a tablet also works well for coding. You can use any browser; I recommend Chrome.

Fig - 1.1: Ticker graph on the search of ticker name Apple Inc

To access the TradingView Platform, you need to sign up at http://tradingview.com. Signing up provides you with a free account that comes with certain limitations. However, most of these limitations can be overcome by learning and utilizing PineScript. Once you have successfully signed up on the TradingView platform, you will have access to various charting tools, the PineScript editor, and cloud storage for saving your programs, all of which are free to use.

After signing up, you can easily search for any ticker symbol on the main page. From there, you have the option to launch a chart. Simply click on the "Launch Chart" button located on the right side of the chart, as indicated in Figure 1.1, and you're good to go!

In the lower bottom portion of the comprehensive chart, as depicted in Figure 1.2, you will find buttons, including the Pine Editor button, along with other useful features.

On the left side of the chart, you will find a range of buttons that serve as drawing tools. These tools allow you to manually draw trendlines, fibo lines, XABCD patterns, Gann patterns, and more. I encourage you to explore and familiarize yourself with these buttons as they provide valuable functionality for your chart analysis and trading strategies. Take the time to learn and utilize these drawing tools to enhance your trading experience.

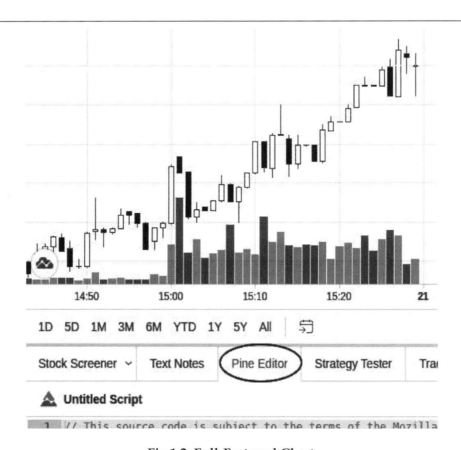

Fig 1.2: Full-Featured Chart

At the bottom of the interactive chart, you will find a tab labeled "PineEditor." This tab allows you to write PineScript codes and instructions directly within the TradingView platform. The best part is that you don't need to install any additional software or set up anything on your computer. The PineEditor tab provides a convenient and accessible space for you to develop your PineScript programs without any hassle.

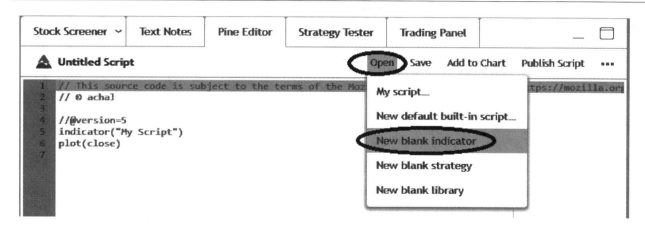

Fig 1.3: Pine Editor with default Blank Indicator Script

To access the Pine Editor for coding purposes, simply click on the "Pine Editor" option. This will open up an editor screen where you can begin writing your code. Alternatively, you can click on the "Open" button and select "New Blank Indicator" to obtain the default indicator script that plots the closing price, as demonstrated in Figure 1.3. In the introduction lesson, we discussed the default code under the listing IN.0.1.

Summary

- TradingView is a free online platform.
- PineScript is cloud-based, eliminating the need for installation.
- You only need a browser to access and use PineScript.
- The full-featured chart in TradingView includes a Pine Editor for running PineScript.
- The full-featured chart also offers various drawing tools for manual chart markings.
- To start coding indicators, you can use the "Blank indicator" option under the Pine Script Editor tab, which provides a default script.

Chapter -2: Your first program in PineScript

In this lesson, you would be writing your first PineScript program and would learn the basics of the PineScript program. The following sections organize the chapter:

- A Simple PineScript Code
- Compiling and running the script
- What are Built-in Functions
- Example of Other Built-in Functions
- What are built-in variables

Pine Editor may be used to practice the codes presented in the examples.

A Simple PineScript Code

In the previous chapter, we learned how to access the "Pine Editor" and open a new blank indicator script. Additionally, in the introduction chapter, we explored the default indicator script. To execute your code, you must add it to the chart. The "Add to Chart" button is located next to the button used to open the new blank indicator script.

Below is the code snippet for LISTING IN.2.1, which you need to enter into your Pine Editor. This code is designed to plot the "close" of the bar on the chart, rather than below it. We have made a modification to the default script by introducing a new parameter in line 5.

INPUT LISTING IN.2.1 Plot value of close on the chart along with candlesticks

```
1: // This source code is subject to the terms of the Mozilla Public License 2.0
2: // © Creating trade Strategies & Backtesting Using PineScript - UDEMY
3:
4: //@version=5
5: indicator("IN.2.1 Plotting Close", overlay=true)
6: plot(close)
```

OUTPUT LISTING IN.2.1

Fig 2.1 is the output display after adding code to the chart. Contrary to listing IN.0.1, where the plot was below the chart, the 'close' values are on the chart.

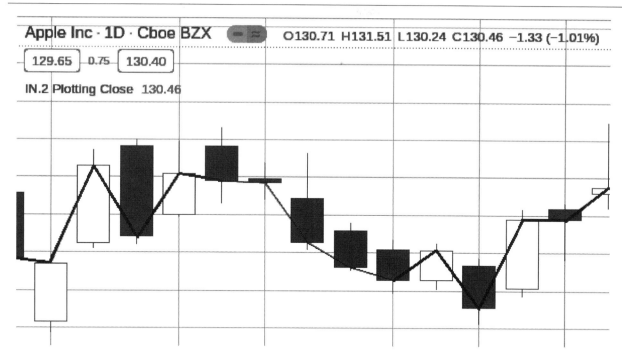

Fig 2.1 Plotting close on chart

ANALYSIS LISTING IN.2.1

The only additional code included in this default code is "overlay=true" on line 5. As discussed in LISTING IN.0.1, lines 1 and 2 are commented out and do not form part of the script. Comments are denoted by two consecutive slashes ('//') and can be used to provide additional information, copyright details, or instructions to programmers for better understanding of the code.

Line 5 specifies the name of the script, which in this case is "IN.2.1 Plotting Close". The script name is enclosed in quotation marks within brackets after the keyword "indicator". The keyword "indicator" indicates that we are creating an indicator and not working on strategies. The "indicator" keyword can accept various inputs in the form of key-value pairs, separated by commas and enclosed in brackets '(..)". One of the mandatory inputs for an indicator is the script's name, also known as the "title". In this case, the script name is "IN.2.1 Plotting Close", as mentioned before.

In the previous example, we had only one input parameter, "title", for the indicator. Now, we have added another input parameter called "overlay" to the indicator, with a value of "true". The "overlay" parameter instructs the system to plot this indicator on top of the existing chart. If we set "overlay" to "false", the plot will be drawn at the bottom of the candlestick chart, similar to how RSI is plotted or as close was plotted in the IN.0.1 example. If we omit this second input for the "indicator", the system will automatically assume the overlay value as "false".

If an input parameter is not provided, the system will make assumptions to prevent the script from crashing. The value that the system assumes in such cases is referred to as the "default value" for that parameter. In the case of the "overlay" parameter, the default value is "false". However, we have the flexibility to modify this value and alter the behavior of the chart.

On line 6, there is an instruction to plot the "close" on the screen. Instead of "close", you can also choose to plot the "high", "low", or "open" values by replacing "close" within the brackets of the plot function. This allows you to plot any of these values according to your preference.

Activity
Try plotting the above code for high or low or open in place of close. Just replace the close with "high" or "low" or "open". You can even do some experiments by replacing close with "(high+low)/2".

Compiling and executing the script

As mentioned earlier, you need to add the code to the chart in order to execute it. The button to add the code to the chart can be found next to the button you used to open the new blank indicator. Once the code is added to the chart, the system compiles the script on the server side. The result of the compilation is then displayed in your browser.

If there is an error during the conversion of script statements into a machine-readable language, known as compilation errors, the console window located just below the pine editor window will display the error message. If you're unable to locate the console window, you can right-click on the top of the pine editor and select "Show Console" as shown in Fig 2.2. This will make the console window visible to view and troubleshoot any compilation errors.

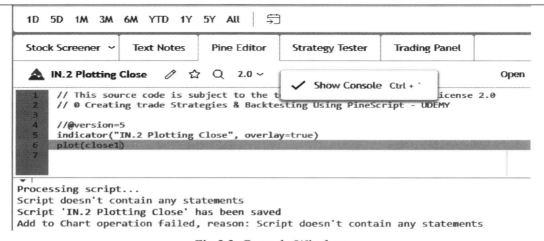

Fig 2.2: Console Window

If there is an error in the code, such as a typo error, the error message will appear in the console window. For example, if I mistakenly type 'close1' instead of 'close' in the code, it will cause the plot function to generate an error. The console window will display the specific error message, allowing you to identify and correct the mistake in your program. You can use these error messages as hints to troubleshoot and fix any issues in your code.

What are the Built-in Functions?

The PineScript language is specifically designed for trading and allows users to code indicators and strategies. However, it is not intended for mathematical modeling of engineering problems or parameter optimization. Different languages and packages have their own focus areas and purposes. For example, MATLAB is commonly used for mathematical modeling, while ASP.NET and PERL are utilized for web development. Similarly, Microsoft Office is primarily used for word processing. Each language is associated with a particular type of activity based on its features, capabilities, and target audience.

In the case of web development languages like ASP.NET and PERL, they come with built-in codes that can be reused by users. These languages have the ability to connect to various database servers and contain specific codes tailored for website-related tasks. By leveraging these pre-existing codes, developers can save time and effort by not having to write every piece of code from scratch.

Likewise, PineScript provides users with built-in functions, which are reusable codes that facilitate faster coding without starting from scratch. These functions calculate various technical indicators such as simple moving averages, relative strength index (RSI), exponential moving averages, and average true range. Users can utilize these functions by providing the necessary inputs, such as the look-back period for RSI calculation and specifying whether to use the bar's close or open values. With just a few inputs, the built-in functions can generate the desired output results. These inputs, known as function arguments, allow users to customize the behavior of the functions and obtain the desired outcomes without having to remember complex formulas or manually write extensive code for each calculation.

```
outputResult = functionName(argument1, argument2, argument3)
```

Inputs to the functions are written after the name of functions inside the brackets and separated by commas. For calculation of Relative Strength Index, built-in-function "ta.rsi" can be used. An example of calculating RSI is given below:

```
myCutomRSI = ta.rsi(close, 14)
```

The function "ta.rsi" is designed to calculate the relative strength index (RSI) and requires two inputs, also known as arguments. The first argument is the source, which represents the data or values on which the RSI calculation will be performed. The second argument is the length or look-back period, indicating the number of periods to consider for the calculation.

In the given code, the variable "myCustomRSI" is used to store the result of the RSI calculation using the "ta.rsi" function. By providing the appropriate source and length values as arguments, the function calculates the RSI and assigns the result to the variable "myCustomRSI". This allows users to store and utilize the calculated RSI value for further analysis or integration into their trading strategies.

In the example LISTING IN.2.1, the "indicator" function is also an inbuilt function indicated by the brackets following its name. It serves as a function that informs the system that the program is intended for creating indicators. The inputs provided to the "indicator" function, such as the script name and the parameter "overlay = true," control the behavior of the indicators on the chart.

Similarly, the "plot" function in line 6 of the previous example is also a function denoted by the brackets following its name. In the previous example, the "close" was used as the input to the plot function, instructing it to draw the closing price on the chart. The "plot" function also accepts other inputs, such as line color, line style, line thickness, etc., which are separated by commas. These inputs determine the appearance of the plotted line. While some of these inputs are optional and have default values, the "source" input, which specifies the data to be plotted (open, high, low, or close), is mandatory for the plot function to draw anything on the chart.

In LISTING IN.2 example, the "close" input in the plot function can be replaced with a custom RSI value to plot the RSI on the chart. Since RSI is typically plotted below the chart, setting "overlay = false" is necessary to draw the RSI below the main chart. The example code below demonstrates this:

INPUT LISTING IN.2.2 Plot value of RSI 7 below the candlestick chart

```
4: //@version=5
5: indicator(title="IN.2.2 Plotting RSI", overlay=false)
6: myCustomRSI = ta.rsi(close, 7)
7: plot(myCustomRSI)
```

OUTPUT LISTING IN.2.2

The RSI calculates in stored in a variable named myCustomRSI. We will be studying more about variables in upcoming chapters. For the time being , you can assume myCustomRSI as a container that is used to store RSI calculated from the function "ta.rsi". The chart at Fig 2.3 provides output after adding the code. The RSI is drawn just below the existing candlestick chart.

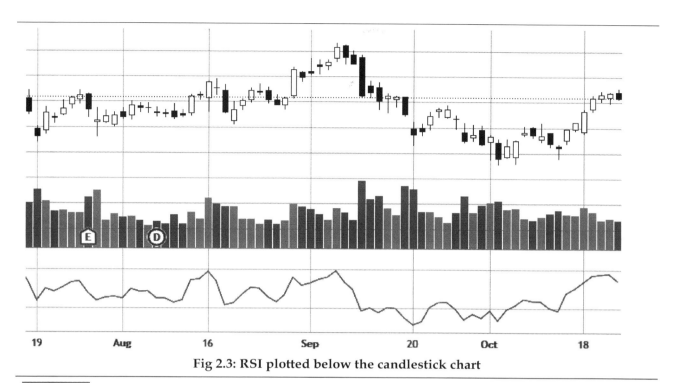

Fig 2.3: RSI plotted below the candlestick chart

ANALYSIS LISTING IN.2.2

In line 5, the "indicator" function is used to create indicators. It takes two arguments (values passed to the function): the script name, which in this case is "IN.2.2 Plotting RSI," and the "overlay" parameter set to "false." By setting "overlay" to "false," we instruct the system to draw the chart below the existing candlestick chart.

At line 6: myCutomRSI = ta.rsi(close, 14)

In this code, the function "ta.rsi" is used to calculate the Relative Strength Index (RSI). It takes two inputs, namely "source" and "length", which represent the data source and the look-back period. The calculated RSI value is stored in the variable "myCustomRSI".

It's worth noting that prior to version 4, the function was simply referred to as "rsi". However, in version 5 and subsequent updates, all technical analysis indicators have been moved to the "ta" namespace, which stands for technical analysis. To access these indicators, you need to use the dot operator on "ta", written as "ta.", followed by the name of the specific technical indicator.

In line 7, the "plot" function is used to plot our custom RSI value, "myCustomRSI", on the chart. By setting "overlay" to "false", the plot is displayed below the main chart.

Example of Other Built-in Functions

As a programmer, it is important to familiarize yourself with the names and functionalities of the built-in functions in PineScript. While it may be challenging to remember the name of every function, having a good understanding of PineScript's capabilities as a programming language is crucial. By knowing the language's capabilities, you can always refer to the PineScript reference manual to find the name and details of specific built-in functions that you need for your program. This allows you to leverage the existing functions rather than writing the entire code from scratch.

In PineScript, there are several standard built-in functions that you may find yourself using frequently. These functions have names that are usually abbreviated versions of their common names, making it easier for you to remember and identify their purpose. By familiarizing yourself with these commonly used functions, you can streamline your coding process and take advantage of the available functionalities within PineScript.

1. EMA: Exponential moving average

   Syntax: ta.ema(source, length) → series[float]

   In simpler terms, the syntax of a programming language refers to the specific format or structure in which a pre-defined function expects to receive input. In the above example, the function requires two inputs in a specific order. The first input is the source data on which the calculation will be performed, typically the closing value of a bar or a time-series data. The second input is the look-back period, determining the number of data points to consider for the calculation. The function then generates a series of float values as its result.

   When working with PineScript, you can calculate an Exponential Moving Average (EMA) simply by calling the appropriate function, as demonstrated in the example below. You don't need to understand the inner workings of the EMA calculation itself; instead, you only need to provide the required inputs and retrieve the output. This abstraction allows you to focus on utilizing the function effectively without delving into the details of its implementation.

   Example: myMA = ta.ema(close,14)

   This function to calculate exponential average takes close as input and calculates EMA for 14 periods. i.e., it would take 'close' values of the last 14 bars for its calculation. The " myMA" variable stores the result of this EMA calculation. The "myMA" is a variable, a container to store value; you can name it anything per your need and convenience. If you reverse the order of arguments provided in the "ta.ema" function, it generates an error. i.e. ta.ema(14,close) would be an error.

2. SMA: Simple Moving Average
   Syntax: ta.sma(source, length) → series[float]
   Example: myMA = ta.sma(close,14)

3. RSI: Relative Strength Index
   Syntax: ta.rsi(source, length) → series[float]
   Example: myRSI = ta.rsi(close,14)

4. ATR: Average True Value
   Syntax: ta.atr(source, length) → series[float]
   Example: myATR = ta.atr(close,14)

5. WMA: Weighted Moving Average
   Syntax: ta.wma(source, length) → series[float]
   Example: myWMA = ta.wma(close,14)

6. MACD: Moving Average Convergence/Divergence
   Syntax ta.macd (source,fastEMA period, Slow EMA period, Signal length)
   Example: [mLine, sLine, hLine] = ta.macd(close, 12, 26, 9)

   The MACD (Moving Average Convergence Divergence) function produces three series variables of type float as its outputs. These variables are the MACD Line, Signal Line, and Histogram Line. The order of the inputs and outputs remains consistent as presented in this book. If you encounter any confusion or need further clarification, you can always refer to the PineScript manual, which is available online as a reliable resource.

7. Rising: Check whether rising for a given period
   Syntax:ta.rising(source, length) → series[bool]
   Example: risingResult = ta.rising(close,5)
   If 'close' for the last 5 bars is rising, the 'risingResult' would be true; else, false.

8. SAR: Parabolic Sar to find potential reversal
   Syntax: ta.sar(start, increment, max) → series[float]
   Example: sarResult = ta.sar(0.2,0.2,0.2)
   This book's upcoming sections provide more details about SAR and its applicability.

Apart from the few common functions discussed above, many built-in functions like ta.nvi(net volume index),ta.obv(on balance volume), ta.pvi(positive volume index), ta.vwap(volume weighted average price), ta.swma(symmetrically weighted moving average),etc make PineScript a language focused on the development of indicators and strategies.

In addition to built-in functions provided by the TradingView platform, you can also define your own function through coding. Defining your function in coding reduces repeatability of code, makes your code clear and more readable and allows you to copy the entire function from a code to use it in other scripts. We would learn to develop functions later in this book.

What are Built-in Variables?

When trading electronically on any exchange, we receive information from the broker or data service provider regarding price, volume, and other tick data. This data includes the current bar's open, high, low, close, and volume, as well as historical data for the bar.

In PineScript, all such information is readily available through built-in variables like open, high, low, close, and volume. The names of these variables clearly indicate the type of data they store. It is important to note that the names of variables, as well as any other variables or functions in PineScript, are case sensitive. For example, using "Close" instead of "close" would create a different variable that the system would not recognize as a built-in variable.

Additionally, you can create your own variables, as we did in previous examples of functions by storing the result value of "ta.sma" or "ta.ema" in a custom variable named "myMA". A variable is a named memory space in the system where we can store data and retrieve it using the variable's name.

Suppose "Karl Marx" lives in your city and you don't know his address, then it would be difficult for you to search for him. If you know the address, you can visit the address and can find "Karl Marx".

Variables can be thought of as references to the data you are storing. When you assign a variable with a name, the system associates that name with a memory address where the data is stored. You can retrieve the data by using the variable name, and the system will locate the memory address associated with that variable and provide you with the data stored there. Built-in variables like open, high, close, etc., serve as references to specific data points. For example, if you request the value of the open variable, the system will access the memory address associated with the open reference and retrieve the corresponding data for you.

It is important to note that you cannot use the variable names of built-in data to assign new values. Since the system already uses those variable names or references to store its own data, it will not allow you to assign different values to them and will produce errors. For instance, trying to write open = close + high would result in an error.

All the built-in variables are "series variables", i.e., they store data in the form of a list. The latest data is written at the end of the list. You can access previous values of such series data by using a [ ] operator.

Data in list variable or "Series Variable" is stored like this:

Value	36.5	36.55	36.45	36.40	36.35	36.40
Bar no	5	4	3	2	1	0
						Recent bar

Fig 2.4: Visual representation of a series variable

Let's say the above data shown is a visual representation for the close. The current bar close can be accessed by close, whereas if you want to access 'close' data for 4 bar back, you can use close[4]. This will be discussed in more detail in upcoming lessons.

Summary

- Errors while running codes are displayed in the console window.
- Built-in functions are the block of reusable code to improve readability, reduce code repetition, and make coding convenient and fast.
- Functions are links to re-usable codes, and inputs to the functions are known as arguments.
- The indicator is a built-in function to create indicators and control their behaviour.
- The argument 'overlay' of the function indicator tells the system about the location of the plot, i.e. on the chart or below the chart. By default, its value is false, i.e. to draw the below chart.

- There are many built-in functions focused on implementing indicators and strategy in PineScript.
- The plot function is used to plot the given dataset on the chart.
- The syntax is a format or a structure into which a pre-defined function can take input and provide output.
- Built-in variables are a series of values wherein the latest being written in last.
- To access a the value of a variable which is 'n' bar behind the current bar, '[ ]' operator is used after the variable's name, and the bar's number is written inside square brackets.

Workshop

To help enhance your understanding of the concepts provided in this chapter, you should try to answer the questions and finish the exercises before you move to the next chapter. The answers and hints to the questions and exercises are given at the back of the book in Appendix A.

Quiz

Q.1 True and False
   A. Can a PineScript compiler see the comments within your Pine program?
   B. The value of close 4 bar back can be accessed using close[4].
   C. The errors generated while executing the script are displayed in the debugging window.

Q.2 Consider fig 2.4; what would be the value of close[0]?
Q.3 Consider fig 2.4. what would be the value of close[1.5]?

Exercises
   1. Modify the program shown in this lesson to plot a simple moving average of 14 periods on the chart.
      (Hint: Use "overlay" to choose the right location for your chart and just replace EMA code with SMA code to the plot)

Chapter -3: Plotting on the Chart

Welcome to Chart Plotting. In this lesson, you will learn the following:

- Moving average crossover
- The plot function
- Arguments for the plot function
- Summary

In the previous three examples, we utilized the plot function to display values for "close" and "RSI" on the chart. Now, let's explore a classic example of a moving average crossover. We will use moving averages - ema 7 and ema 14 and plot them both on same chart.

Moving Average Crossover

Moving average crossover is a classic example of a fundamental trading strategy. As novice coders, I encourage you to give this code a try on your Pine editors.

INPUT LISTING IN.3.1 Plot value of EMA 7 and EMA14 on the candlestick chart

```
1: // This source code is subject to the terms of the Mozilla Public License 2.0
2: // © Creating trade Strategies & Backtesting Using PineScript - UDEMY
3:
4: //@version=5
5: indicator("IN.3.1 EMA crossover", overlay=true)
6: myEMA7 = ta.ema(close, 7)
7: myEMA14 = ta.ema(close,14)
8: plot(myEMA7)
9: plot(myEMA14)
```

OUTPUT LISTING IN.3.1

Both moving averages have been plotted on the chart in **Fig IN.3.1**, and we can also observe the crossover. However, both lines are of the same color, making it difficult to distinguish between the slow-moving average and the fast-moving average.

No other arguments were provided to the plot function, so the plot function used a default color for both lines. This issue can be resolved by adding additional arguments to the plot function. In the next section, we will learn about additional arguments for plot functions that can modify the behavior of the plot lines.

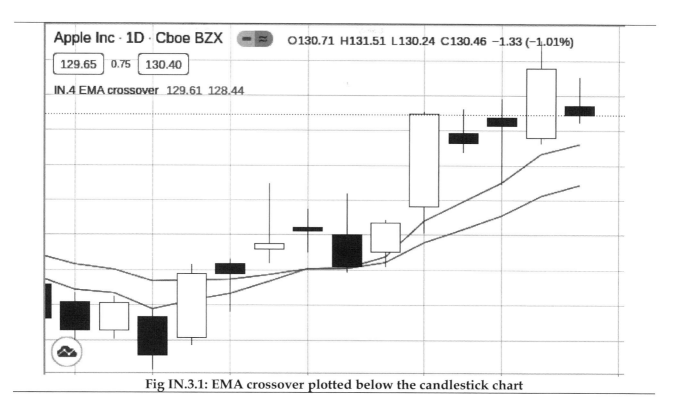

Fig IN.3.1: EMA crossover plotted below the candlestick chart

ANALYSIS LISTING IN.3.1

Every aspect of the code has already been covered in previous lessons. In this code, we utilized overlay = true to enable plotting on the candlestick chart instead of below it. Furthermore, in lines 8 and 9, we employed the "plot" function twice to generate two distinct EMA lines on the chart.

The plot function

In the plot function, we have only provided one argument, which is the EMA value. However, the "plot" function offers several other optional arguments that can modify the behavior of the plotted line, such as color, thickness, or style.

The syntax of the plot function with some primary optional arguments is as follows:

plot(series, title, color, linewidth, style, offset) → plot

There are more arguments that the plot function can accept, but I have kept it limited here to help you understand without overwhelming you with too many inputs. Even experts don't use all the optional arguments at once. If you're interested in exploring the other optional arguments of the plot function, you can always refer to the PineScript reference manual available on the TradingView website. Now let's discuss each input of the plot function in detail.

Arguments to the plot function

series: This is the data source to be plotted. In the previous case, it was the "myMA" series. This input is compulsory for a plot function. The series input is mandatory for plotting because it serves as the fundamental data source that forms the basis of the plot. It's like the building blocks that allow the plot function to create meaningful visual representations. Without the series input, there would be no data to plot, and the plot function would be left empty-handed, trying to draw something out of nothing.

title: "title" is the name you wish to give to the plot series. Here you can define them as "EMA 7" or "EMA 14", as the case may be. Below is an example:

plot(myEMA7,title="EMA7")

There is a comma between the first and second arguments. You can either write title=" EMA7", or if you are using the same order of argument as provided in the syntax statement above, you can also write it as:

plot(myEMA7,"EMA7")

Both statements will yield the same result. However, being a forgetful human with a less-than-perfect memory, I can never seem to remember the correct order in which arguments should be provided for any function. That's why I prefer using the argument name followed by an equal sign and then the corresponding value. For example, title="EMA7" assigns the value "EMA7" to the argument named "title". The equal sign (=) is used to assign the value to the argument. The "title" argument can be named anything and can even be omitted if desired.

Now, the million-dollar question is: why is EMA7 in quotes ("") and not written as title=EMA7? The answer is that EMA7 is a name, an alphanumeric value. Therefore, it needs to be written within quotes. Additionally, the title argument expects an alphanumeric input. So, even if I want to name the plot as 001, it has to be provided as "001".

color: As the name implies, it determines the color of the line plotted on the screen. It accepts a color value as input. There are two ways to define color values. You can use constants like 'color=color.red' or create them using the "color.new" function. When using constants for colors in PineScript, you have a range of options available, including color.aqua, color.black, color.blue, color.fuchsia, color.gray, color.green, color.lime, color.maroon, color.navy, color.olive, color.orange, color.purple, color.red, color.silver, color.teal, color.white, and color.yellow.

PineScript provides predefined color constants for various colors. For example, if you want to use the color blue, you can use the color constant "color.blue." Similarly, if you want to use red for an object, you can use the color constant "color.red." Personally, I have a fondness for the color brown. However, one limitation of PineScript is that it does not have a predefined color constant for brown. So, what if a user wants to use a custom color for their object? Can we define a custom color? PineScript offers two functions as a solution for custom colors.

1. color.new() function

2. color.rgb() function

The color.new() and color.rgb() functions are both used to define custom colors. However, we have two functions for the same purpose because they accept different formats for color values, and each format has its advantages.

The color.new() function allows you to specify color codes as hex values. This means you can provide the color using a hexadecimal parameter or by using a color constant like color.blue or color.red. If you're unsure about the hex color code for any of your favorite colors, a quick Google search can help you find it.

On the other hand, the color.rgb() function allows you to specify colors using RGB numbers. RGB stands for red, green, and blue, which are the primary colors used to create various shades. By providing specific values for each of the RGB components, you can create custom colors.

In summary, the difference between color.new() and color.rgb() lies in the format of the color values they accept. color.new() accepts hex values, while color.rgb() accepts RGB numbers. Let's first understand the syntax and example for these functions:

	color.new()	color.rgb()
Syntax:	color.new(colorConstant, transp)	color.rgb(r,g,b,transp)
Brown Color:	color.new(#964B00,50)	color.rgb(150,75,0,50)
Range of transp	0 to 100	0 to 100

The color.new() function accepts two arguments: the color constant and the transparency value. The color constant can be specified as a hex parameter or using predefined color constants like color.blue or color.red. If you're unsure about the hex color code for your favorite colors, a quick Google search can help you find them.

Another parameter that can be used with the color.new() function is transparency, which represents the level of "look through" or opacity. In previous versions, the "transp" parameter was used in functions like plotshape() and other object drawing functions. However, in version 5, it has been dropped and incorporated into the color.new() and color.rgb() functions to make colors transparent. The transparency parameter can take values from 0 to 100. A value of 0 means the color will be solid, completely blocking any objects behind it. On the other hand, if a value between 0 and 100, such as 50, is used, objects behind the color will appear but with some blurring or transparency.

The second function, color.rgb(), can accept four values as input: the values for red, green, blue, and transparency. The values for red, green, and blue can range from 0 to 255, representing different intensities of each color. Transparency, as discussed earlier, can range from 0 to 100. By combining these three color components, the color.rgb() function can create a wide range of custom colors. If you want to delve deeper into the RGB color scheme, you can search the internet for more information.

To add color to our EMA line example, you have multiple options. You can use the following syntax:

1. Using named arguments:
plot(myEMA7, title="EMA7", color=color.red)

2. Using positional arguments:
If you know the order of arguments, you can write:
plot(myEMA7, "EMA7", color.red)

3. Using color argument without title:
You can also use the color argument without the title argument:
plot(myEMA7, color=color.red)

The choice is yours because the "title" argument is optional. Feel free to use the method that is most convenient for you.

linewidth: As the name implies, it is used to adjust the thickness of a line. It accepts integer values as input, such as 1, 2, 3, or 4. However, it does not accept decimal values like 1.5 or 2.3. The default value set by the system is 1. This means that if no argument is provided to the plot function for linewidth, the system will assume a value of 1.

To change the color and thickness of the EMA line, you can use the following code:

```
plot(myEMA7,title="EMA7",color=color.red, linewidth=2)
```

In the code above, the linewidth argument is set to 2, which will make the line thicker than the default value of 1. Feel free to adjust the linewidth value according to your preference to achieve the desired thickness for the EMA line.

Note that in the case of numeric values and constants like color constants, there is no need to use quote marks (" ").

style: The style argument in the plot function allows users to customize the appearance of the plotted line. It offers various options such as continuous lines, dotted lines, histogram representation, and more. By specifying the desired style, you can modify the visual presentation of the line on the chart.

The available values for the style argument include plot.style_line, plot.style_stepline, plot.style_histogram, plot.style_cross, plot.style_area, plot.style_columns, and plot.style_circles. The default value is plot.style_line, which represents a continuous line.

You don't need to remember all the available styles or colors. It's sufficient to be familiar with commonly used styles. If you ever feel unsure, you can always refer to the PineScript reference manual, which is available online.

In the code provided below, you can see the style argument along with other optional arguments:

```
plot(myEMA7, title="EMA7", color=color.red, linewidth=2, style=plot.style_stepline)
```

Alternatively, you can omit the other optional arguments and simply specify the style:

```
plot(myEMA7, plot.style_stepline)
```

Feel free to experiment with different variations of style in your Pine editor by adding the script to the chart. This will allow you to visualize and understand the effects of different style choices.

offset: The offset parameter allows you to shift the plot to the left or right by a specified number of bars. By default, the offset is set to 0, indicating no shift. However, in certain cases, such as identifying pivot points or swing highs/lows, it may be necessary to adjust the plot by a few bars.

For instance, when marking pivot points, it is common for the pivot to be identified one or two bars after it occurs. In order to accurately plot or mark these points, we may need to shift the line or marker by one or two bars to the left. To achieve this, negative values can be used for offset, which shifts the plot to the left. Conversely, positive values would shift the plot to the right.

In the examples provided in this guide, I only utilize the necessary arguments of PineScript. I focus on the arguments that are relevant to the specific topic being discussed.

In the previous listing, IN.4, we plotted a crossover using two different EMAs. However, both plots had the same color, making it difficult to distinguish between them. To address this issue, the code has been modified as follows:

```
8: plot(myEMA7,color=color.green)
9: plot(myEMA14,color=color.red)
```

You can use your ideas, try different combinations of arguments in the plot to observe the resultant plot.

Fill function

The fill function is used to highlight the area between two lines or plots. The general syntax of the fill function is as follows:

```
fill(line or curve first,line or curve second,color,title)
```

INPUT LISTING IN.3.2 plot value of SMA 7 and SMA14 and fill area between them

```
01: //@version=5
```

```
02: indicator("IN.3.2 Example Fill",overlay=true)
03: SMA7 = ta.sma(close,7)
04: SMA14 = ta.sma(close,14)
05:
06: plot1= plot(SMA7)
07: plot2=plot(SMA14)
08:
09: fill(plot1,plot2,color=color.new(color.blue,75))
```

OUTPUT LISTING IN.3.2

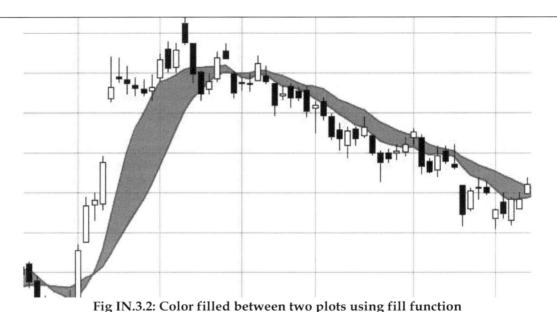

Fig IN.3.2: Color filled between two plots using fill function

ANALYSIS LISTING IN.3.2

In the provided code, we have utilized the plot function to draw two plots representing the 7-period SMA (Simple Moving Average) and 14-period SMA. These plots are assigned to variables named "plot1" and "plot2" respectively, on lines 06 and 07.

To highlight the area between these two plots, we use the fill function on line 09. The fill function takes the values of the two plots, "plot1" and "plot2", as arguments. By utilizing these values, the fill function fills the area between the two plots with a designated color or shading, creating a visual representation of the enclosed region.

Furthermore, it's important to note that the color.new() function has been employed in the provided code. This function allows us to define custom colors with a specific level of transparency.

In the code, a transparency value of 75 has been set, which means that the highlighted portion will have a certain level of opacity. As a result, the bars and objects located behind the colored highlighted area will still be visible, albeit with some degree of transparency. This enables us to visually distinguish the highlighted region while maintaining visibility of the underlying chart elements.

Example using fill function

In this example, our objective is to highlight a region of volatility determined by the Average True Range (ATR) indicator. We will create two plots: one by adding the ATR value to the close price, and the other by subtracting the ATR value from the close price.

To provide a visual indication of the highlighted region, we will offset the plots by one bar into the future. This offset allows us to make informed decisions when the price approaches the upper or lower boundary of the ATR value plot.

Ultimately, we will utilize the fill function to highlight the area between the two plots, creating a visual representation of the region of volatility.

`INPUT` LISTING IN.3.3 plotting upper and lower ATRs and fill area between them

```
01: //@version=5
02: indicator("Example Fill",overlay=true)
03: atr7 = ta.atr(7)
04:
05: plot1= plot(close+atr7,offset=1)
06: plot2=plot(close-atr7,offset=1)
07:
08: fill(plot1,plot2,color=color.new(color.blue,75))
```

When the price reaches the highest or lowest value of the 7-period Average True Range (ATR), we can expect some significant movement in the market. In the provided code, the plot is based on a daily chart, but it's interesting to note that the plot is shifted one day ahead.

This shift is done because the ATR calculation requires complete information about each trading day. After the trading day ends, we can analyze the expected trading range for the next day. By shifting the plot one day into the future using the "offset" property, we can better understand and visualize the potential trading range with this time adjustment.

`OUTPUT` LISTING IN.3.3

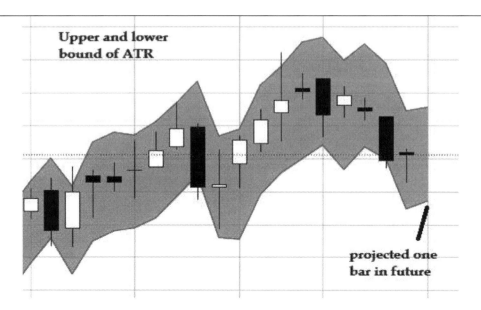

Fig IN.3.3: Color filled between upper and lower bounds of ATR

ANALYSIS LISTING IN.3.3

The code calculates the 'average true value' (ATR) for the last seven periods at line 3 and stores the value in a variable called "atr7". The "ta.atr" function is used to calculate ATR, and it requires only one argument, which is the look-back period for the calculation.

In lines 5 and 6, plot functions are used with an offset of 1, which shifts the entire plot one bar into the future. If a negative value is used as the offset, the plot would shift backward instead. At line 8, the fill function is used to fill the gap between the two plots, creating a visual highlight of the region.

Summary

- Plot functions have several optional arguments that can be used to customize the appearance of the plot.
- Not all optional arguments are necessary to execute the plot. You can choose to provide only the arguments that you need.
- Each argument has specific input requirements. For example, the title argument can take any name or input, the color argument can use color constants, the linewidth argument only accepts positive integers, and the style argument has predefined inputs defined by PineScript.
- The color.new function allows you to create custom colors with transparency. The transparency value (transp) can range from 0 to 100.
- The offset argument can be used to shift the plot forward or backward by a positive or negative integer value.

- Multiple plot functions can be called within a script to create multiple plots on a chart.
- The fill function can be used to highlight the region between two lines or plots.
- For further information on additional arguments of any function, you can refer to the Pine reference manual available on the TradingView website.

Workshop

To help enhance your understanding of the concepts provided in this chapter, you are encouraged to answer the questions and finish the exercises before you move to the next chapter. At the back of the book, in Appendix A, are answers and hints for the exercises and questions.

Quiz

1. Is this correct: plot(myEMA7,title="EMA7",color=color.red,linewidth=2.5)
2. Is this code correct:
   plot(myEMA7,Title="EMA7",color=color.red,linewidth=2)
3. Is this code correct:
   plot(myEMA7,"EMA7",color.red,linewidth=2)

Exercise

1. Write a script to plot "SMA" of 3, 7, and 14 periods wherein the colour of all three lines should be different. 14-period SMA should be most thick, followed by 7 and 3 periods.
2. Write a script to plot rsi with 14 and 7 periods and fill in the gap between them. Make sure that the plot is made below the chart by setting overlay=false. The function to calculate RSI is ta.rsi, which can take two values as input, i.e. series and look-back period. You may calculate rsi on close for 14 days by using ta.rsi(close,14).

Chapter -4: Understanding Data Types

In the previous chapter, we explored the functionalities of inbuilt and plot functions, which allowed us to customize and display data on charts. Now, we'll delve into the fundamental concepts of storing data in variables, declaring variables, and naming them. The chapter is divided into following sections:

- Concept of DataType
- Concept of Variable
- Arithmetic Operations in Series Variables
- Accessing historical prices
- Summary

Concept of DataType

In nature, we encounter a wide variety of objects and materials that require different methods of storage. For example, we use bottles to store liquids like oil and water, containers or bags to hold grains in the kitchen, and pen drives to save data when working from home. We can consider these objects as storage devices, each designed for a specific purpose.

However, we cannot interchangeably use these storage devices for different types of objects. We cannot store kitchen oil in a pen drive or save data in a bottle. Why is that?

The reason lies in the specific characteristics of each object. Kitchen oil is a liquid, and it requires a container specifically designed to hold liquids safely. On the other hand, a pen drive is designed to store digital information in the form of data files, not liquids. The structure and functionality of a pen drive are tailored to handle digital data, not physical substances like oil.

Similarly, in computer programming languages, we encounter different types of information or data, each with its own specific properties. To store and handle this information effectively, we need to use appropriate data storage mechanisms based on the type of data involved. We must consider factors such as the data's structure, format, and intended use.

By understanding the nature of the data and selecting the appropriate storage methods or variables, we can ensure efficient and accurate handling of information in computer programming. Just as we choose the right storage containers in our everyday lives, we must make informed choices when it comes to storing and managing data in computer systems.

Information that we may require to store in programming may have:

1. Whole numbers : The whole numbers are known as Integers. example: 1, 2, 3, 4, etc
2. Decimal Numbers : In computer language, decimal numbers like 1.1, 1.4, 2.6, etc., are also called float numbers.

3. Alphanumeric : We may also have names like James, Kitty, Dolly, Rosy, and Ammie. These names or any alphanumeric name are known as string
4. Boolean : Some of the information is stored in the form of "yes" and "no" only. Such type of information is known as "Boolean" in computer language.
5. Date : the date is another special type of data.

For each of the above five types of information, we have five different types of containers or information holders to store. The classification of information by its type is called datatype. We may, therefore, have five primary datatypes in pinescript.

DataType	Example
INTEGERS	509, 430, 600
FLOAT	509.4, 430.6, 600.5
STRING	Ammie, JOJO, 500MG
BOOLEAN	TRUE or FALSE
DATE	28 JULY 2010

We need to select suitable datatype for storage of our information so that
- we can store information
- we can store complete information
- we use minimal resources for storage
- we can operate on data when required.

We take an example of choosing the correct DataType

Problem Statement: You are tasked with storing information about the number of guests who dined at a restaurant. What data type should you use?

Considering that the information will consist of whole numbers, as guests are counted in whole units and cannot be fractions like 2.5, we have a few options to choose from: integer, float, and string data types.

Using the string data type may not be suitable for this scenario. Arithmetic operations cannot be performed on string values. For example, if you want to divide the number of guests by the number of days, it would be impossible to do so if the number of guests is stored as a string. The system would treat the numbers as words, and division between words is not possible, resulting in an error. Additionally, if you were to store the numbers 9 and 10 as strings and perform addition, the result would not be 19. Instead, the system would either refuse to perform the operation or concatenate the two strings, resulting in "910" instead of the expected sum.

Using the float data type, you could store the guest information as 2.0, 3.0, or 56.0, with a zero after the decimal point. While this approach would work for practical purposes, it would utilize additional system resources unnecessarily, which is not ideal for efficient programming.

It's important to note that you cannot perform arithmetic operations or other operations between data of different types. For example, you cannot add a number to a string, date, or boolean value. Similarly, there are some limitations on operations between integers and floats.

Considering these factors, the most appropriate data type for storing the number of guests who dined at your restaurant would be the integer data type. This data type allows you to represent whole numbers accurately and efficiently, enabling you to perform arithmetic operations and other calculations seamlessly.

In this lesson, we have discussed a few data types, in reality, pinescript has many data types, and when we encounter any such new data type in this book, it will be discussed.

Concept of Variable

In the previous section, we learned about the importance of choosing the appropriate data type to store information. A data type is a classification that categorizes information based on its characteristics. Just like we choose a specific container, such as a bottle or mug, to store a new liquid material, we need to select the right data type to store different types of information.

A variable serves as a container for storing information. It can be assigned any data type according to our requirements. Whether it's an integer, float, boolean, or date, a variable can hold and manipulate data as needed. It can be emptied, overwritten, and reused multiple times.

In the case of storing the number of guests, we determined that the appropriate data type is an integer. However, before using a variable, it's essential to give it a meaningful name for identification purposes. As programmers, we usually choose names that are easy to remember and provide hints about the information stored in the variable.

For instance, I can name the variable "numberofGuest," "guestNo," "nguest," or simply "guest," depending on my preference. It's generally recommended to use camelCase when naming variables, which involves writing phrases in a way that each word or abbreviation starts with a capital letter, without any spaces or punctuation in between. For example, "smaLength," "buySignal," or "numberGuest." In larger projects, it can be helpful to use prefixes for certain types of variables to make them more easily identifiable. The following prefixes can then be used:

- i_ for variables initialized through input() calls, the input() function would be discussed later in the book. In simpler terms, all input data from a user.
- c_ for variables containing colours.
- p_ for variables used for the plot.

- Constants in upper case (in caps). Constants are initialized at the beginning of scripts, and the value of these variables does not change during execution. For example, PI = 3.14

Points to note:
- Try avoiding variable names longer than 8 characters.
- Variable names are case sensitive, i.e. variable "close" is not the same as "Close".
- Never name a variable with any keyword being used by the system. A keyword is a word or variable name or function name used by the system for built-in functions and variables — for example, ema, sma, bar, high, low, volume, close. The system does not accept naming variables with keyword names as they are already used by the system.

Arithmetic Operations in Series Variable

In TradingView, most values are represented as series, which means they consist of a list of values that correspond to the number of bars on the chart. For example, the 'close' series contains a specific 'close' value for each bar on the chart.

The built-in variables in TradingView, such as open, high, low, close, and volume, as well as derived variables like hl2, hlc3, ohlc4, and other calculations involving series variables, all have values represented as series.

Let's consider the calculation of the range, which is defined as the difference between the high and low values of a bar (range = high - low). Since this calculation involves a series of floating-point numbers, the output will also be a series of floating-point numbers. The representation of this range calculation is shown below:

Bar no	5	4	3	2	1	0
High	90.1	90.5	90.45	91.2	91.5	92.4
Low	89.2	88.2	89.5	89.8	90.3	91.3
Range	0.9	2.3	0.95	1.4	1.2	1.1

In pinescript, the calculation of range can be done by simple one line code i.e. Range = high-low, when a statement is executed in Pine Script, the calculation is not performed only for the current bar. Instead, it is carried out for all bars on the chart, and the resulting values are stored in a new series variable corresponding to each bar. Therefore, you can access specific values from the series using indexing, such as retrieving the value of the range 4 bars ago with range[4].

You don't know how to access value of an variable for historic bar ? you can do this by using a square bracket with name of the variable, the value of the range at 4 bars back can be accessed by using the expression range[4]. This is possible because the range, like other variables in Pine Script, is represented as a series.

Accessing Historical Data

To calculate a simple moving average (SMA) for 7 periods, we need the 'close' data of the current bar and the previous 6 bars. You can access the historical data of any series, including the 'close' data, by using the square bracket [ ] operator with the index of the desired bar inside the brackets. The close[0] or simply close provides value of current bar and close[1] provides value of close for one time period back. The 'close[0]' or simply 'close' provides the value of the current bar, while 'close[1]' provides the value of the close for the previous time period.

For this example, we manually calculate the SMA by adding up the 'close' values of the current and previous 6 bars, and then dividing the sum by 7. By accessing the historical 'close' data using indexing, we can perform this calculation for each bar on the chart and plot the resulting SMA series. This approach allows us to have SMA without relying on built-in functions like ta.sma().

How do we calculate a simple average?

To calculate the simple moving average (SMA) for seven periods, add all the close values for the current and past six periods, and divide the sum by seven. The instruction code in pinescript would look like this:

```
SMA7 = (close[0]+ close[1]+ close[2]+ close[3]+ close[4]+ close[5]+ close[6])/7
```

In this code, we create a variable SMA7 and add up the close values for the current bar (close) and the previous six bars (close[1] to close[6]). Then, we divide the sum by seven to calculate the SMA, and assign it to the variable SMA7.

INPUT LISTING IN.4.1 Calculating SMA without built-in function.

The complete code to plot the sma7 using above method without using the inbuilt function ta.sma() is given below:

```
01: //@version=5
02: indicator("Historical Data Example",overlay=true)
03: // SMA7 calculation
04: SMA7 = (close[0]+close[1]+close[2]+close[3]+close[4]+close[5]+close[6])/7
05: plot(SMA7)
```

ANALYSIS LISTING IN.4.1

Line 01: //@version=5: This specifies the version of the Pinescript that the code is written in.

indicator("Historical Data Example", overlay=true): The code at line 02 sets the name of the indicator to "Historical Data Example" and sets the overlay to true, which means the indicator will be plotted on the main chart.

// SMA7 calculation: This is a comment and not part of the code

SMA7 = (close[0] + close[1] + close[2] + close[3] + close[4] + close[5] + close[6]) / 7: This line calculates the SMA7 by adding the close value of the current bar (close[0]) and six previous bars and then dividing the sum by 7.

plot(SMA7): This last line of the code plots the calculated SMA7 on the chart.

Compare the result obtained from the above code with the plot generated from the function ta.sma(). Do you find any difference?

Summary

- Datatypes are based on the classification of information
- Operation between two different data types is neither allowed nor desirable.
- Built-in variables in pinescript are series variables.
- Variable names are case sensitive. Keywords should not be used as a variable name.
- It is recommended to use camelCase for the naming of a variable.
- Most of the variables in pinescript are series variables, i.e. each value with the corresponding bar

---

Quiz

Q1. The data type of HL2 inbuilt variable is:

    1. Integer   2. Float   3. Series   4. Float Series

Q2. If X = close[1.6] instruction is given, what would be stored in X:

    1. Value of close one bar ago   3. Value between one bar and two bars, depending on input, i.e. 1.6 in this case.

    2. Value of close two bar ago   4. Error

Q3. Suppose X = 1.1 and Y = 2, if Y:=X instruction is given, Y would be

    2   2.0   1   1.1

4. You want to store information on the number of guests dined at your Restaurant in the last 30 days. What data type should you use:

    1. Integer   2. Float   3. Float Series   4. Integer series

5. Which of the following statements accurately describes the calculation of a simple moving average (SMA) for seven periods?

A) The SMA is calculated by adding the close values of the current bar and the previous six bars, and then dividing the sum by 6.

B) The SMA is calculated by multiplying the close values of the current bar and the previous six bars, and then dividing the product by 7.

C) The SMA is calculated by adding the close values of the current bar and the previous six bars, and then dividing the sum by 7.

D) The SMA is calculated by subtracting the close values of the current bar and the previous six bars, and then dividing the difference by 7.

Exercise

Q1. You want to store details of rainfall per day in your city for 365 days. You would be required to calculate the average rainfall for 365 days. What data type variable would you use to store rainfall?

Chapter -5: Operators in PineScript

Operators in a programming language are like special symbols that allow us to perform different actions on numbers or information. Just like we use math symbols like plus, minus, multiplication, and division in everyday life, programming has its own set of symbols that let us do similar things with numbers and data.

For example, if you want to add two numbers together, you would use the plus symbol (+) as an operator in programming. Similarly, you can subtract numbers with the minus symbol (-), multiply them with the asterisk symbol (*), or divide them with the forward slash symbol (/).

But operators in programming aren't just limited to math. They can also be used to compare values or perform logical operations. For instance, you can check if one number is greater than another using a comparison operator. You can also combine conditions using logical operators like "and" or "or" to make more complex decisions in your programs.

In the upcoming sections, we will explore different types of operators and learn more about how they work and what tasks they can help us accomplish in programming.

- Assignment Operator
- Arithmetic Operator
- Comparison Operator
- Logical Operators
- Identifying Doji
- Drawing Shapes on Chart

Assignment Operator

Before we move on to other operators, let's explore the assignment operator, which you have already encountered in previous chapters.

In PineScript, the "=" operator is known as the assignment operator. Its general form is as follows:

left-hand-operand = right-hand-operand

In this statement, the assignment operator instructs the system to assign or write the value of the right-hand operand to the memory location associated with the left-hand operand. After the assignment, the value of the left-hand operand will be equal to the value of the right-hand operand.

To clarify, the left-hand operand should be a variable capable of storing the assigned value. It should have the appropriate data type for the value being assigned.

For example, the statement "length = 5;" assigns the value of 5 to the variable "length." The value of "length" will now be 5.

In your previous lessons, you calculated the Exponential Moving Average (EMA) and stored it in the variable "myMA" using the assignment operator. The statement "myMA = ta.ema(close, 14);" assigns the calculated EMA value to the variable "myMA".

It's important to note that both the left-hand operand and the right-hand operand of the assignment operator should have the same data type. When assigning a value to a variable for the first time, the "=" operator automatically sets the data type of the left-hand operand based on the data type of the right-hand operand.

If you are reassigning a value to an existing variable, it is recommended to use the ":=" operator instead of "=" to ensure proper reassignment. Also, when reassigning a value, make sure that the data type of the reassigned value matches the data type of the variable.

Keep in mind that the left-hand operand must be a variable with a data type compatible with the assigned value. For instance, writing an expression like "6 = length" is incorrect because the assignment operator works from right to left, and the left-hand operand should be a variable capable of receiving the value from the right-hand operand.

If the left-hand operand is not previously used or defined in the code, the system will automatically assign the data type of the left-hand operand based on the data type of the right-hand operand or value.

Arithmetic Operators

There are five arithmetic operators in Pine Script as the name suggests, they do addition, subtraction, multiplication, division, and modulo operator to calculate the remainder after division.

+	Addition	*	Multiplication
-	Subtraction	/	Division
%	Modulo (remainder after division)		

These operators operate on integers and float datatypes. The data-type of a resultant depends on the data-type of operands. In case you are unfamiliar with the modulo operator, it is an operator that provides a reminder after division. For example, 15%12 means reminder after 15 is divided by 12; the answer would be 3. Below are example to refresh all these operators :

Addition (+): The addition operator is represented by the plus symbol (+) and is used to add two numbers together. For example, a + b would give the sum of variables a and b.

Subtraction (-): The subtraction operator is represented by the minus symbol (-) and is used to subtract one number from another. For example, a - b would give the difference between variables a and b.

Multiplication (): The multiplication operator is represented by the asterisk symbol () and is used to multiply two numbers. For example, a * b would give the product of variables a and b.

Division (/): The division operator is represented by the forward slash symbol (/) and is used to divide one number by another. For example, a / b would give the quotient when variable a is divided by variable b.

Modulo (%): The modulo operator is represented by the percent symbol (%) and is used to calculate the remainder after division. For example, a % b would give the remainder when variable a is divided by variable b.

Comparison Operators

There are six comparison operators in Pine Script. As their name suggests, these operators are used to compare values or operands. The result of a comparison operator is always either "true" or "false", which can be stored in a boolean variable.

<	Less Than	!=	Not Equal
<=	Less Than or Equal To	==	Equal
>	Greater Than	>=	Greater Than or Equal To

Let's use an example to determine whether a candle is an up candle or not.

We can use the comparison operator ">" to compare the close price of the candle with its open price: **upCandle = close > open**

The comparison "close > open" evaluates to either "true" or "false", and this result is stored in the boolean variable upCandle. If upCandle is "true", it means the candle is a green candle (an up bar). If upCandle is "false", it means the candle is a red candle (a down bar).

Comparison operators in programming allow us to ask questions or make comparisons. The computer provides us with an answer in the form of "yes" or "no" (or "true" or "false"). In this case, we are asking the computer whether the close price is greater than the open price, and it responds with either "true" or "false" to indicate the result.

Logical Operators

There are three logical operators in Pine Script:

not	Negation	or	Logical Disjunction
and	Logical Conjunction		

"and" Operator: The "and" operator is represented by the keyword "and" and is used to combine two conditions. It returns "true" only if both conditions are true. For example, condition1 and condition2 would evaluate to "true" if both condition1 and condition2 are true.

Let's say you want to go for a walk, but you have two conditions that need to be met before you can go. The conditions are:

- It is not raining.
- The temperature is between 60 and 80 degrees Fahrenheit.

To check both conditions using the "and" operator, you can use the following statement:

```
if (not raining) and (temperature >= 60 and temperature <= 80):
    go for a walk
else:
    stay indoors
```

In this example which is not a real pinescript code and only used for demonstration, the "and" operator is used to combine the two conditions. The first condition checks if it's not raining (using the "not" operator to negate the condition). The second condition checks if the temperature is between 60 and 80 degrees Fahrenheit. Both conditions need to be true for the program to execute the "go for a walk" statement. If any of the conditions is false, the program will execute the "stay indoors" statement.

So, in simpler terms, the "and" operator helps us check if multiple conditions are true at the same time before making a decision or taking an action.

"or" Operator: The "or" operator is represented by the keyword "or" and is used to combine two conditions. It returns "true" if at least one of the conditions is true. For example, condition1 or condition2 would evaluate to "true" if either condition1 or condition2 (or both) are true.

Let's consider another scenario where you want to go out, but you have two possible conditions that would allow you to go. The conditions are:

- It's a weekend.
- You have finished all your work for the day.

To check both conditions using the "or" operator, you can use the following statement:

```
if (weekend) or (workFinished):
    go out
else:
    stay indoors
```

In this example, the "or" operator is used to combine the two conditions. The first condition checks if it's a weekend, and the second condition checks if you have finished all your work for the day. If either of the conditions is true (or both), the program will execute the "go out" statement. If both conditions are false, the program will execute the "stay indoors" statement.

So, in simpler terms, the "or" operator allows us to check if at least one of multiple conditions is true before making a decision or taking an action. If any of the conditions is true, it considers the overall condition as true.

"not" Operator: The "not" operator is represented by the keyword "not" and is used to negate a condition. It returns the opposite of the condition. For example, not condition would evaluate to "true" if condition is false, and vice versa.

Logical operators are used for comparing two booleans; the result is a boolean. Study the below code.

```
upCandle = close > open
upVolume = volume > volume[1]
Res1 = upCandle and upVolume
```

The "upCandle" and "upVolume" are boolean variables that store their results as either true or false. In the statement "Res1 = upCandle and upVolume," the operation on the right-hand side involves two boolean variables with a logical operator in between them. With the AND operator, the result (stored in "Res1") will be true only if both boolean operands are true. In other words, "Res1" will be true only if the bar is an up-candle and its volume is higher than the volume of the previous bar.

Result Table for AND operator

Operant 1	Operant 2	Result
True	True	True
True	False	False
False	True	False
False	False	False

If we change the logical operator to "or", i.e. Res1 = upCandle or upVolume, it will allow Res1 to be true if any of the operands is true.

```
upCandle = close > open
upVolume = volume > volume[1]
Res1 = not upCandle and not upVolume
```

Result Table for OR operator		
Operant 1	Operant 2	Result
True	True	True
True	False	True
False	True	True
False	False	False

In the above example, Res1 would be 'true' only if the bar is not an uptick and its volume is less than the volume of the previous bar. The "not" logical operator is applied to a single operand and checks whether the value is false or true. If the operand is false, it returns true; otherwise, it returns false.

Result Table for NOT operator	
Operant	Result
True	False
False	True

The NOT operator reverses the value in the result; a "true" becomes "false", and "false" becomes "true".

Identifying Doji

In this section, we will create and explore a script to identify and analyze a doji pattern. The doji pattern is a frequently observed pattern in candlestick charts, widely used in technical analysis.

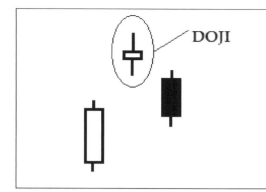

	The doji formation is characterized by the opening and closing prices being nearly equal. However, some traders prefer to consider additional characteristics when identifying a doji pattern. These additional criteria may include a smaller price range, higher volume for the doji compared to the previous bar, and other factors. By incorporating these extra characteristics, traders can refine their doji pattern analysis and potentially gain further insights from the candlestick chart.

In LISTING IN.5.1, the code is designed to identify a doji based on the characteristic that the opening and closing prices are almost equal. However, in practical terms, it is rare for the open price of a bar to be exactly equal to the close price. Therefore, it is advisable to introduce a tolerance value or a range within which we consider the opening and closing prices to be "almost equal" for identifying a doji candlestick pattern.

By incorporating a tolerance value, we can define a range within which the difference between the open and close prices is considered small enough to qualify as a doji. This allows for a more flexible and practical approach in identifying doji patterns in real-world candlestick charts.

In the code, you would need to modify the condition that checks for the near equality of the open and close prices to account for the tolerance range. The specific value for the tolerance would depend on the specific requirements and preferences of the analysis being performed.

INPUT LISTING IN.5.1 Identifying Doji on a candlestick chart

```
1: // This source code is subject to the terms of the Mozilla Public License 2.0
2: // © Creating trade Strategies & Backtesting Using PineScript - UDEMY
3: //@version=5
4: indicator("Tutorial Doji",overlay = true)
5: //Doji open = close
6: //ideally, open can never be equal to close, take 0.05 % as tolerance
7: //Revised condition for DOJI, i.e. open is almost equal to close within the tolerance
8:
9: tolerance = 0.05/100
10: Is_OC_Equal = (open > close  and open < close*(1 + tolerance)) or (open < close and open > close*(1-tolerance))
11:
12: plotshape(Is_OC_Equal, color = color.blue, style = shape.circle, location = location.abovebar) // plot circle
```

The above code is used to identify potential doji candles, and it includes a tolerance of 0.05%. This means that the code considers a candle to be a potential doji if the difference between the opening and closing prices is within 0.05% of each other.

OUTPUT LISTING IN.5.1

The code provided in the book identifies doji candles based on the specified criteria and marks them with a blue circle. However, in the print version of the book, it may not be possible to visually identify the blue color. To see the blue circle, you would need to run the code on your computer or device, where the blue color will be displayed as intended.

Fig IN.5.1: Doji marked with a blue circle

ANALYSIS LISTING IN.5.1

Line 1 to 2 and 5 to 7 are all commented and is not part of the code. Line 3 has version of the script, i.e. 5. Line 4 has an indicator function with the indicator's name and overlay value as 'true'.

Line 9 defines a variable tolerance, an acceptable difference between close and open prices to consider them almost equal. It is defined here as 0.05%, i.e. 0.05/100

The code at line 10 introduces a boolean variable called "Is_OC_Equal" on line 10. This variable evaluates two conditions and stores the results as either true or false.

The first condition, (open > close and open < close*(1 + tolerance)), checks if the open price is greater than the close price and if the open price is within the tolerance range above the close price. This condition is used to identify down bars (red candles) where the open price is slightly higher than the close price. For example, if we have an open price of 100.2 and a close price of 100.1, the first condition would be true, indicating a down bar.

The second condition, (open < close and open > close*(1 - tolerance)), checks if the open price is less than the close price and if the open price is within the tolerance range below the close price. This condition is used to identify up bars (green candles) where the open price is slightly lower than the close price.

If either of these conditions evaluates to true, it means that the open and close prices are nearly equal, and the "Is_OC_Equal" variable becomes true, indicating the presence of a doji where the open and close prices are very close to each other.

Overall, the code determines if a candle qualifies as a doji based on the provided criteria and sets the boolean variable "Is_OC_Equal" accordingly.

The challenge lies in marking the doji on the chart. We cannot directly use the plot function because it requires a series of values for plotting. To address this, we utilize a specific built-in function called "plotshape()" on line 12. This function enables us to draw shapes on the chart. More information about the "plotshape()" function and its usage will be covered in detail in the upcoming section.

Drawing Shapes on Chart

In Pine Script, both the plot() and plotshape() functions are used to visualize data on the chart, but they have different purposes and functionalities.

plot() Function: The plot() function is primarily used to plot numerical values, such as indicators or calculated data points, on the chart. It takes a series of values and plots them as a line or a histogram. It is commonly used for displaying indicators like moving averages, oscillators, or custom calculations. The plot() function is suitable for visualizing continuous data points over a specific time period.

plotshape() Function: On the other hand, the plotshape() function is used to plot shapes or symbols on the chart rather than numerical values. It allows you to mark specific events or patterns with visual symbols such as arrows, circles, crosses, triangles, and more. This function is handy for indicating specific conditions or patterns like doji candles, trend reversals, or specific chart patterns or marking buy or sell events.

Thus, the key difference between the plot() and plotshape() functions in Pine Script is that plot() plots numerical values as lines, while plotshape() plots shapes or symbols on the chart for marking specific events or patterns.

The format or syntax of plotshape() and its arguments may be written as:

> plotshape(boolean condition, color = color constant, style = shape name, location = above or below)

The first input is a boolean condition; if the condition is true, then only the plotshape function would execute; otherwise, nothing would be drawn. Under IN.5.1 line 12, we have already used this function as:

> **plotshape(Is_OC_Equal, color = color.blue, style = shape.circle, location = location.abovebar,)**

Here, "Is_OC_Equal" is a boolean variable that acts as a condition; the shape is plotted when "Is_OC_Equal" is 'true'.

Under the "style" arguments, we may define the shape we want to draw. The function "plotshape()" offers the following shapes for plotting:

Shape Name	Shape	Shape Name	Shape
shape.xcross	✕	shape.arrowdown	⬇
shape.cross	✚	shape.square	◼
shape.circle	●	shape.diamond	◆
shape.triangleup	▲	shape.labelup	🔺
shape.triangledown	▼	shape.labeldown	🔻
shape.flag	⚑	shape.arrowup	⬆

Learning each shape is unnecessary; you may learn two or three shapes you like and feel would be used more frequently.

Another argument for the function is color. We have previously discussed color in the previous chapter in relation to the plot function. You can customize the color of the marks in the plotshape function using either the "color.new" function or predefined color names provided by the system.

In Pine Script version 5, the system offers predefined color constants that you can use. These include color.aqua, color.black, color.blue, color.fuchsia, color.grey, color.green, color.lime, color.maroon, color.navy, color.olive, color.orange, color.purple, color.red, color.silver, color.teal, color.white, and color.yellow. These constants represent specific colors that you can use to specify the color of the plotshape marks.

Alternatively, you can also use hexadecimal color codes like #ff001a or #ffffff to define any color you desire. Hex color codes provide a wider range of color options and allow for more precise color customization.

By utilizing either the predefined color constants or hexadecimal color codes, you can define the desired color for the plotshape marks and add a visual element to your chart based on your preferences.

Another argument that this function can take is location; it may have several values, but for all practical purposes, remember these two:
- location.abovebar — above bar.
- location.belowbar — below bar.

The property of transparency can be added to shapes using the color.new function in Pine Script. In previous versions of Pine Script, the transparency property was an argument called "transp" in the plotshape function. It had a value ranging from 0 to 100, where 0 meant fully visible and 100 meant completely invisible.

However, in Pine Script version 5, the transparency property has been removed from the plotshape function and has been incorporated into the color.new function. With color.new, you can specify the desired transparency level using transp property.

For example, to set a shape color with 50% transparency, you can use color.new with the desired RGB values and specify the transparency by setting it 50. A lower "transp" value will make the shape more opaque, while a higher value will make it more transparent.

By utilizing the color.new function and adjusting the alpha channel, you can control the transparency of the shapes in your chart, allowing you to achieve the desired visual effect with transparency in Pine Script version 5. We have already studied color.new() function in chapter 3.

```
plotshape(Is_OC_Equal, color = color.blue, style = shape.circle, location = location.abovebar, )
```

The above statement asks the system to draw a small circle-shaped mark in blue above the bar when the condition, i.e. boolean variable "Is_OC_Equal", is 'true'.

There are a few other functions for text drawing (plotchar) and arrow drawing (plotarrow), which are discussed below for reference.

Drawing Text on Chart

In the last section, we studied about plotting of shapes on a chart. Suppose you like to write "D" on the bar or you want to write "B" or "S" text on the chart above or below a bar, then function plotshape() cannot be used. In place of plot shape, you can use a plotchar() function.

The word "char" is a short form for the word character. This function is capable of printing one character. The plotchar() function's syntax is similar or almost identical to the plotshape(), except for the "style" argument. Here in the place of the "style" argument, we have to use the "char" argument to supply characters for printing on a chart.

```
indicator("Tutorial Doji",overlay = true)
tolerance = 0.05/100
Is_OC_Equal = (open > close  and open < close*(1 + tolerance)) or (open < close and open >
    close*(1-tolerance))
plotchar(Is_OC_Equal, char = 'doji', location = location.abovebar)
```

The plotchar function cannot write the complete text "Doji". The space above the bar is so tiny that only one char can be written. In the above example, an attempt has been made to print the "doji" word; however, the result shown below only produces char "d" above the bar.

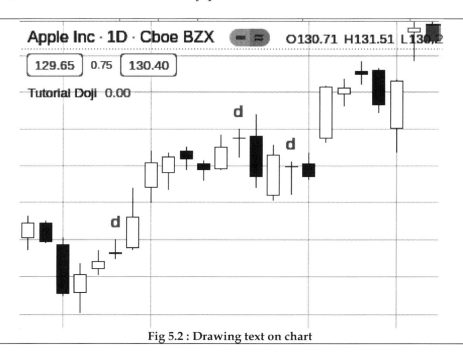

Fig 5.2 : Drawing text on chart

The plotchar() function can also be used to print various ASCII or Unicode symbols like ❄, ♥, ☀, €, ⚑, ★, etc.

In addition to the previously mentioned functions, the plotchar() function can also be utilized for debugging purposes in Pine Script. Although we won't be using it in the current context, it's worth noting its concept for future reference. For instance, if you encounter difficulties in identifying doji patterns and wish to examine the difference between close + tolerance and open, you can employ the plotchar() function.

Indeed, it is quite common to encounter situations where the result of a script does not align with our expectations. In such cases, it becomes essential to identify the source of the error or problem. This process of locating and resolving issues within a script is known as "debugging" in programming terminology.

Debugging involves systematically analyzing the code to identify any logical errors, syntax issues, or unintended behaviors that may be causing the unexpected results. It often requires careful examination of variables, data flows, conditional statements, and the overall program logic.

```
plotchar((close*(1+tolerance))-open,title="value",char="",location=location.belowbar)
```

The above code would print nothing on the chart as char ="", but values shall appear under the data window on the right pane of the chart.

Fig 5.3 : Data Window

Under the data window, you can see that "value" appears under tutorial doji. As you move your cursor on a new bar, the value automatically changes, which might help you in your debugging process. These values are otherwise not available for viewing.

Drawing Arrow on Chart

If you need to display an arrow on the chart, the plotarrow() function is suitable for this purpose. The syntax of plotarrow() is similar to plotshape(), except for the "style" argument, which is not required because the arrow style is predefined. Another irrelevant argument in plotshape() is "location", which is not needed for plotarrow().

Additionally, since the color of the arrow differs depending on whether it is an up arrow or a down arrow, two more arguments, "colorup" and "colordown," have been added to plotarrow() to specify the respective colors. It's important to note that plotarrow() cannot accept a Boolean as a series input for plotting; it requires a float series.

Due to these modifications in the function's arguments, the syntax for using plotarrow() has changed. Here is the revised syntax for your reference:

Syntax: plotarrow(series[float], colorup=[color constant], colordown=[color constant])

Below is the revised doji example:

```
//@version=5
indicator("Tutorial Doji",overlay = true)
tolerance = 0.05/100
Is_OC_Equal = (open > close  and open < close*(1 + tolerance)) or (open < close and open >
    close*(1-tolerance))?1:-1
plotarrow(Is_OC_Equal, colorup=color.teal, colordown=color.orange)
```

The plotarrow function is used to display arrows on the chart, and its output is shown below. The input source for this function should be a float or an integer with positive and negative values. An up arrow is drawn for all positive values, while a down arrow is drawn for all negative values.

To accommodate this behavior, a slight code change has been made. The variable "Is_OC_Equal" is now defined as an integer instead of a Boolean. When the condition is true, a value of 1 is stored in the "Is_OC_Equal" variable. In the case of false, a value of -1 is stored.

The specific operator used for this conversion, which transforms the true/false values into -1 or 1, will be discussed in upcoming sections. For now, there is no need to worry about the details of that statement.

By incorporating this code change and based on the conditions defined in the script., the plotarrow function can effectively display up arrows for positive values and down arrows for negative values on the chart.

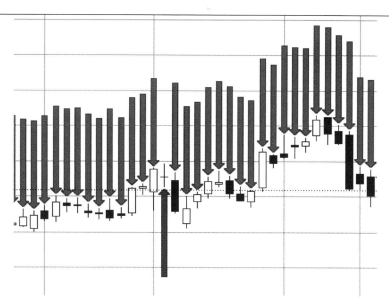

Fig 5.4 : Drawing Arrows

You can also plotarrow by just giving one argument to the plotarrow function, as all other arguments are optional.

```
plotarrow(Is_OC_Equal)
```

By default, the up arrow is displayed in green, while the down arrow is shown in red. However, you have a preference for using the plotshape() function with style=shape.arrowdown or shape.arrowup to draw arrows on the chart.

Below is the code to plot the RSI on the chart with overlay=true. The RSI values are subtracted from 50, so that values below 50 are considered as 'negative', and values above 50 are treated as 'positive'. The length of the arrow on the chart corresponds to the strength of the negative or positive value.

INPUT LISTING IN.5.2 : Plotting RSI on graph using arrow function

```
//@version=5
indicator("RSI Overlay Example", overlay=true)

rsiValue = ta.rsi(close, 14)
rsiOffset = rsiValue - 50

// Plotting arrows based on RSI offset
plotarrow(rsiOffset)
```

OUTPUT LISTING IN.5.2

In the provided output, it is apparent that the lengths of the bars or arrows vary. When the RSI offset has a higher negative value, the down arrows appear longer. Conversely, when the RSI offset has a more positive value, the up arrows appear longer.

This variation in length is intentional and corresponds to the strength of the negative or positive values in the RSI offset. It provides a visual representation of the magnitude or intensity of the negative or positive sentiment indicated by the RSI.

The purpose of this visual distinction is to allow for easier identification and interpretation of the strength or intensity of the RSI offset. By observing the lengths of the bars or arrows, one can quickly assess the degree to which the RSI offset deviates from the threshold of 50.

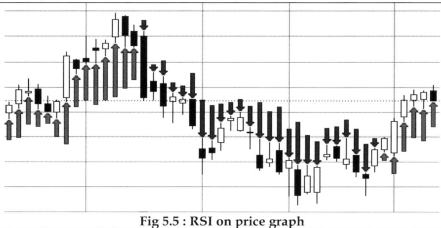

Fig 5.5 : RSI on price graph

Can you think of a way to mark only those bars with RSI below 20 and above 80?

Marking Engulfing Bar

An engulfing bar is a type of candlestick pattern characterized by a bar that has both a higher high and a lower low compared to the previous bar. This means that the price range of the engulfing bar completely engulfs or encompasses the price range of the preceding bar.

In simpler terms, for an engulfing bar to form, the high of the current bar must be higher than the high of the previous bar, and the low of the current bar must be lower than the low of the previous bar. This signifies a significant shift in market sentiment and can indicate a potential trend reversal or continuation.

The engulfing bar pattern is widely used in technical analysis as it provides insights into the strength and momentum of price movements. Traders and analysts often consider engulfing bars as potential signals for entering or exiting trades, depending on the prevailing market conditions and the presence of other confirming indicators or patterns.

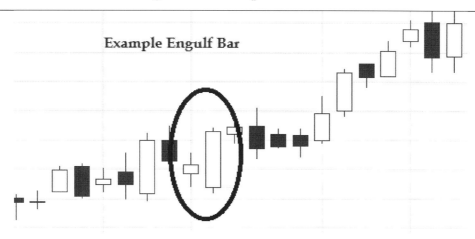

Fig 5.6 : Engulting Bar

Let's identify the "engulf" bar using pinescript script. Below is the code for identification of engulfing bar.

INPUT LISTING IN.5.3 : Identifying Engulf Bars

```
01: //@version=5
02: indicator("Engulf Example",overlay=true)
03: engulf = high > high[1] and low < low[1]
04: plotshape(engulf,text='engulf')
```

OUTPUT LISTING IN.5.3 : Identifying Engulfing Bars

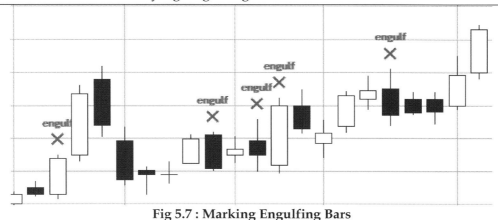

Fig 5.7 : Marking Engulfing Bars

ANALYSIS LISTING IN.5.3

The The condition for an "engulf" is specified in line 3 of the code. It states that the current high must be higher than the previous high, which is obtained using square brackets with an index of 1. Similarly, the current bar's low should be lower than the previous bar's low, accessed using the notation low[1].

Both of these comparison conditions yield either true or false results. Only when both conditions are true, the value of the variable "engulf" will be true. This means that for a bar to be considered engulfing, it must satisfy both criteria simultaneously. i.e. the high of current bar should be higher and low of current bar should be lower than the last bar.

For example:

engulf = high > high[1] and low < low[1]
if only high > high[1] is true and low < low[1] is false, the expression shall become like this:

engulf = true and false

and the result of "engulf" would be false

engulf = false.

The value of "engulf" can only become 'true' when both the conditions are 'true'. Why are both conditions required to be 'true' before the result can be true? The answer is that both logical conditions are joined with logical operator AND. If it had been joined with the OR logical operator, the engulf would have become true when any condition becomes true.

In the plotshape() function, an additional argument called "text" has been utilized. This argument allows for the inclusion of text beside the shape mark on the chart. It provides the capability to add descriptive labels or annotations to the plot.

In this particular instance, the text argument is used to display the word "engulf" beside the cross mark. This helps to visually label the specific pattern being identified on the chart, providing additional information and clarity for interpretation.

Can you improve the above code? Can you add additional instructions for the identification of the trend? Can you refine the engulf and only mark those that can provide potential reversal? Try using volume, trend, RSI, and EMA to improve the code.

Marking Morning Doji Star

The morning Doji Star is a bulling candlestick formation. It consists of a three-candle pattern that typically occurs during a downtrend, indicating a potential trend reversal or a bullish reversal signal.

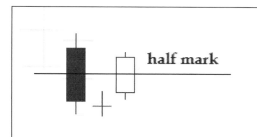	The formation starts with a long bearish candle, representing selling pressure and a continuation of the existing downtrend. The second candle is a small-bodied Doji candle, characterized by its open and close prices being nearly equal. The Doji candle signifies indecision and suggests a possible weakening of selling pressure.

The third candle is a strong bullish candle that opens higher than the Doji's high and closes near or above the midpoint of the first bearish candle. This bullish candle confirms the reversal in sentiment, with buying pressure overpowering the selling pressure.

The Morning Doji Star formation is considered a reliable bullish signal, indicating that the market sentiment has shifted from bearish to bullish. Traders often look for this pattern as a potential entry point for long positions, as it suggests a potential upward movement in the price.

However, it is essential to validate the Morning Doji Star pattern using other technical analysis tools or indicators to confirm the reversal before making trading decisions.

INPUT LISTING IN.5.4 : Identifying Morning Doji Star

```
//@version=5
indicator("Morning Doji Star Example",overlay=true)
range1 = high - low
tolerance = 0.09/100

candle1 = math.abs(close[2]-open[2])/range1[2] > .6 and close[2] < open[2]
candle2 = (open[1] > close[1]  and open[1] < close[1]*(1 + tolerance)) or
  (open[1] < close[1] and open[1] > close[1]*(1-tolerance)) and close[1] < (close[2]+range1[2])
candle3 = close > open and close > (close[2]+range1[2])

MDS = candle1 and candle2 and candle3
plotshape(MDS,text='MDS',offset=-1,location=location.belowbar)
```

Below is the output on SBIN daily chart from the NSE exchange. One such pattern has been found.

OUTPUT LISTING IN.5.4 : Identifying Morning Doji Star

Fig : 5.8 – Morning Doji Star

The Morning Doji Star is a relatively uncommon pattern that appears on a price chart. It is not advisable to trade based solely on the presence of a Morning Doji Star. Instead, it is recommended to consider additional factors and indicators before making trading decisions.

One crucial aspect to consider when trading the Morning Doji Star is its alignment with the support line. The presence of the pattern along the support line adds further confirmation to its potential bullish reversal signal. By aligning the Morning Doji Star with the support line, traders can enhance the reliability of the pattern and increase the likelihood of a successful trade.

In addition to the Morning Doji Star, there is also a similar pattern known as the Evening Doji Star. This pattern follows a similar three-candle structure but appears during an uptrend, indicating a potential bearish reversal.

To increase the identification of such patterns, traders can make adjustments to the parameters used to scan for them. By fine-tuning the parameters, one can potentially identify more instances of Morning Doji Stars or similar candlestick patterns, providing more opportunities for analysis and trading decisions.

It is important to approach these patterns with caution and use them as part of a comprehensive trading strategy that incorporates other technical analysis tools, indicators, and risk management principles. Relying solely on the presence of a Morning Doji Star or any individual pattern without proper analysis may lead to unreliable or inconsistent trading outcomes.

Summary

- Assignment operator rewrites, change the value of the left side variable of the operator with the right side of the operator.
- The result of an arithmetic operator is a number, which could be integer or float depending on the type of operands.
- The result of the comparison operator is always boolean. i.e. true and false
- Operands of Logical Operators are boolean, and the result is also a boolean.
- The function "plotshape()" is used for plotting the shape above/below any bar.
- The function "plotchar()" is used to plot a character on the chart like "B", "S", or "D". The value of the plotchar() condition can also be accessed from the data window of tradingview.
- The function "plotarrow()" is used to plot an arrow in the chart.

Quiz

Q.1 In the statement PI = 3.14, what is the datatype of PI?

Q.2 Consider the following statements:

```
PI = 3.14
X = 4
Result = X > PI and X < 10
```

What would be the value of the Result?

Q.3 Consider the following statements

```
PI = 3.14
X = 4
Result = X > PI or X > 10
```

What would be the value of the Result?

Q.4 What would be 13 % 5?

Q.5 What does this code try to find by storing the result in condition?

```
mySMA = ta.sma(close,14)
Res1 = close > mySMA
Res2 = close[1] < mySMA
condition = Res1 and Res2
```

a.   Breakout condition
b.   Crossover of SMA by price

Exercise

Q.1 In the statement

```
PI = 3.14
result = PI => 4
```

What would be the result after correcting the error? Why has this error appeared?

Q.2 Improve doji pinescript code by including EMA 50. If the close of doji is above EMA 50, put a red down triangle above the bar. If the close of doji is below EMA 50, put a green up triangle below the bar.

Q3. Write a code to identify and mark an inside bar. An inside bar is a bar which has a lower high and high low as compared to the previous bar.

Chapter -6: Control-flow: Iteration

The In programming, the statements in your source files are typically executed in a sequential manner, from top to bottom, in the order they appear. However, control flow statements allow you to break this sequential flow and introduce decision-making, looping, and branching capabilities. This enables your script to execute specific code blocks conditionally, depending on certain conditions or requirements.

To understand control flow, let's consider an analogy with reading a book. When you read a book, you start from page one and continue reading page by page until you reach the end of the book. The logical order of the book ensures that you read each chapter in sequence. However, in some situations, you might need to read chapter 5 before chapter 1 or chapter 2. Similarly, in programming, control flow statements provide the ability to repeat certain tasks or skip specific statements based on different conditions.

There are two main types of control flow statements:

Looping Statements: These statements allow you to repeat a specific set of tasks or statements multiple times. They are useful when you need to iterate over a collection of data, perform calculations, or execute a block of code a certain number of times. Examples of looping statements include "for" loops, "while" loops, and "do-while" loops.

Branching Statements: These statements enable you to branch off the sequential flow of statements based on certain conditions. They allow you to make decisions in your code and execute different code blocks depending on the evaluation of those conditions. Branching statements include "if-else" statements, "switch" statements, and "conditional" statements.

By using control flow statements effectively, you can design your code to handle different scenarios, make decisions based on specific conditions, and create more dynamic and flexible programs. The following upcoming sections will delve deeper into these concepts and provide a better understanding of control flow in programming.

- Flow Chart
- Repeating task
- The for-loop statement
- The while loop statement

Flow Chart

According to the definition provided by Wikipedia, a flowchart is a specific type of diagram that visually represents a workflow or process. It serves as a graphical depiction of an algorithm, which is a step-by-step procedure for solving a particular task or problem.

In essence, a flowchart presents information through various shapes, symbols, and arrows, illustrating the sequence of steps or actions involved in a process. It provides a clear and visual representation of how tasks are interconnected and executed within a system or procedure.

By utilizing different symbols and connectors, a flowchart helps to illustrate the logical flow of activities, decision points, loops, and other key elements of a process. It enables individuals to understand the structure and progression of a task or workflow, facilitating better communication and analysis. (2)

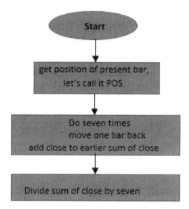

Fig: Flow diagram for average

The flowchart depicted above outlines the step-by-step process for calculating an average or simple moving average. Flowcharts serve as valuable tools for conveying information and facilitating understanding, even for individuals without technical expertise.

Now, the next step is to translate this flowchart into a program or set of instructions that a computer can comprehend. You can refine the flowchart into a more technical format, resembling the following example of a technical flowchart:

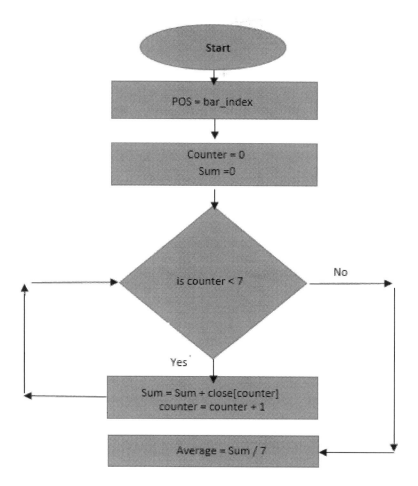

Fig: Flow chart with loop

This technical flowchart represents the same steps as the previous flowchart but in a format that aligns with programming concepts. It serves as a guide for converting the logical steps into specific instructions that a computer can execute.

By transforming the flowchart into a technical form, you establish a foundation for writing the program or code that will implement the steps outlined in the flowchart. This allows you to communicate the process to the computer effectively and enable it to perform the desired calculations.

Through this conversion process, you bridge the gap between the flowchart's visual representation and the technical implementation required to execute the algorithm or process.

Here, POS is the current position of the bar. In PineScript, the inbuilt variable bar_index is used to provide the bar's position. The first bar of the chart is numbered as zero, and all subsequent bars are numbered relative to the first bar. However, you may also use your counter for counting the number of bars and the "[ ]" operator to access previous bars. Counters are used in loop statements to repeat certain statements a specific number of times. In our algorithm, we have to keep summing close for the last 7 bars. It means that we are repeating one step 7 times. In such a scenario, we use a loop statement.

In the above flow chart, we have defined two variables, one is the counter to keep count of the number of steps, and another is the sum to store the sum of closes. The counter is an integer datatype with one increment (therefore, counting cannot be like 1, 2, 2 and a half, quarter to 3 and three), and the sum is a float datatype.

The loop statement starts with a condition, which, when true, a particular set of steps is repeated. If the condition is false, we come out of the loop and complete the remaining statements.

In the loop, the condition statement should become false at some point in time; otherwise, the program would keep on running for infinity, utilizing all the resources.

In the given flowchart, there is a condition statement "counter < 7". If this condition evaluates to true, certain statements will be repeated. If it evaluates to false, the system will exit the loop and proceed to calculate the average.

The purpose of the counter variable is to keep track of the number of steps or iterations performed. The initial value of the counter is set to zero before entering the loop.

One of the statements that will be repeated 7 times is "counter = counter + 1". This statement increments the counter by 1 in each iteration, effectively counting the number of times the loop has been executed.

Inside the loop, there is another statement "sum = sum + close[counter]". This statement calculates the sum by adding the value of the "close" data at the position indicated by the current value of the counter. In the first iteration (when the counter is 0), the expression "close[counter]" represents the current bar's "close" value.

By executing "sum = sum + close[counter]", the right-hand side of the equation is evaluated and the result is stored in the left-hand side variable "sum". In the first loop, where the counter is zero, the sum is initially zero, so the statement becomes "sum = 0 + close[0]". This adds the value of the close for the current bar to the sum.

This process is repeated for each iteration of the loop, gradually accumulating the sum of the "close" values from the previous 7 bars.

By using the counter variable and accessing previous bar values with square brackets, you can perform calculations that involve historical data and accumulate the necessary information to calculate the average or perform other analysis.

Let's assume the close values for the last 7 bars are: 10, 9, 10, 9, 8, 7, and 8, with 10 being the most recent close value and 8 being close[6].

When the first iteration of "sum + close[0]" is executed, the initial value of sum is 0, and the value of close is 10. The result of adding 0 and 10 (close[0]) is 10, which is then stored in the sum variable. This statement allows for cumulative summation.

Now let's focus on the statement "counter = counter + 1". This is an assignment statement, where the right-hand side is evaluated and the result is assigned to the left-hand variable. In the first iteration, the counter variable is initially set to 0. So, when we evaluate "counter + 1", the right-hand side becomes 1, and this value is stored in the counter variable on the left side of the equals sign. This type of statement is known as an increment statement, as it increases the value by one.

After executing both statements within the loop, we move on to the second iteration. The loop condition "counter < 7" is checked, and since the counter is now 1 (which is less than 7), the loop continues and the statements inside the loop are executed again.

In the second iteration, the statement "sum = sum + close[counter]" is evaluated. The current value of sum is 10 (from the previous iteration), and close[1] is 9 (the value of close one bar back). The result of adding 10 and 9 is 19, which is then stored in the sum variable, following the cumulative sum formula. The next statement, "counter = counter + 1", increments the counter to 2.

The loop continues in a similar manner, with the counter increasing by one in each iteration and the sum accumulating the cumulative sum of close values.

At the end of each iteration, we have the following values:

Loop 1: counter = 0, sum = 10
Loop 2: counter = 1, sum = 19
Loop 3: counter = 2, sum = 29
…
This process continues until the loop condition "counter < 7" becomes false, at which point the loop exits and we have the final sum value calculated.

When the counter becomes 7, it is no less than 7, and the loop condition becomes false. The program exits from the loop to continue to execute those statements that are to be executed on the comparative condition being false. i.e. average = sum/7 is executed, and the result is stored in a new variable average.

In the given scenario, the bar position variable (POS = bar_index) appears to be redundant and unnecessary. This is because we have effectively managed the tracking of bars using the "counter" variable in our algorithm. Therefore, we can remove the POS = bar_index statement from the flowchart and the program, as it serves no practical purpose and consumes additional resources.

It is crucial to have a clear understanding of the algorithm before starting the coding process. Developing a comprehensive algorithm provides insights into the program flow, loops, conditional checks, and other essential aspects.

For individuals who are new to programming and coding, it can be beneficial to create a variables chart. This chart helps in visualizing and keeping track of the variables and their values as the program progresses through each iteration of the loop. By updating the variables chart at every loop iteration, you can effectively monitor the changes and ensure the accuracy of your program.

Taking a structured approach, such as creating an algorithm and maintaining a variables chart, can enhance your understanding of the code and enable you to write more efficient and error-free programs. An example is shown here:

Loop condition	Counter	Sum	Average
-	0	0	-
0 < 7	1	10	-
1 < 7	2	19	-
2 < 7	3	29	-
3 < 7	4	38	-
4 < 7	5	46	-
5 < 7	6	53	-
6 < 7	7	61	-
7 < 7	7	61	8.71

Creating such tables in the initial learning phase could help you a lot.

Repeating task

After reviewing the aforementioned flowchart example, it becomes evident that the task of adding past close values to the sum variable needs to be repeated until a certain length is reached in order to calculate the average.

The flowchart illustrates the looping structure required to perform this task. The loop condition checks whether the counter is less than the desired length. If it is true, the statements inside the loop are executed, which include adding the close value to the sum variable and incrementing the counter.

INPUT LISTING IN.6.1 Calculating SMA using a loop

```
1: // This source code is subject to the terms of the Mozilla Public License 2.0
2: // © Creating Trade Strategies & Backtesting Using PineScript - UDEMY
3: //@version=5
4:indicator("IN.6 SMA using loop",overlay = true)
5: sum = 0.0
6: for counter = 0 to 6
7:    sum:= sum + close[counter]
8: SMA7 = sum/7
9: plot(SMA7,color=color.yellow)
```

OUTPUT LISTING IN.6.1

The plot in fig IN.6 is result obtained when the code is applied to the stock of Apple (AAPL) for plotting simple moving average for 7 periods calculated using loop statements. If you want to cross-check the result, you may plot a simple moving average using the "ta.sma" function plot(ta.sma(close,7),color=green)

It produces the same simple moving average (SMA) values as those generated by the built-in function specifically designed for calculating the SMA. This indicates that the code successfully implements the logic of calculating the SMA by summing up the desired number of close values and dividing the sum by the specified period.

Fig IN.6.1: SMA calculated using a loop

ANALYSIS LISTING IN.6.1

Line 6 contains a "for" loop statement; this statement keeps a count of loops and repeats the statement(s) written below the "for" statement with indentation, i.e. 4 spaces or one tab at the beginning of a line. Only in line 7 does the statement "sum:= sum + close [counter]" have space at the beginning of the line; therefore, only line 7 is going to be repeated by the "for" loop statement.

The 'sum' is a mutable variable, and a new value can be given to it by an operator ':=' in the body of the loop. Mutable variables are those variables that can be rewritten. We use the ":=" operator to rewrite a variable's value instead of the "=" operator. If a variable is being used or assigned for the first time, we use the "=" mark. This enables the system to judge the variable's datatype and accordingly assign memory size and address of the location where the value would be stored.

Line 8 calculates the average by dividing the sum of close for the last seven bars by seven.

The "for" loop statement

Looping or iteration is a fundamental concept in programming that allows a set of statements to be executed repeatedly until certain conditions are satisfied. One type of loop commonly used is the "for loop," which controls the execution of either a single statement or multiple statements identified by indentation (typically 4 spaces or one tab).

The syntax of a "for loop" consists of three parts: a counter variable, a range that specifies the lower and upper limits for the counter, and an incremental step. This structure defines how many times the loop will iterate and provides control over the execution flow. A basic "for loop" follows the format:

```
for X = 0 to 6  by 1
    sum:= sum + close[X]
```

In the provided example, the variable X is used as a counter, with a range of "0 to 6" and a step of "1".

When a "for" loop is initialized, the counter is set to the first number in the range, which in this case is 0. The program then executes all the statements indented below the "for" statement. Once it reaches the last statement within the indented block, the program returns to the "for" statement and increments the counter by the specified step value. In this example, the counter X would be incremented to 1 on the second iteration, 2 on the third iteration, and so on.

To modify the increment value of the counter variable, you can change the step value in the "for" statement. For example, if you use a step of 2, the counter X would increase from 0 to 2, then to 4, 6, 8, and so on. By default, if the step is not specified, it is assumed to be 1. In this case, if "by 1" is not included in the "for" statement, the program will still use the default step value of 1, and there would be no difference in the iteration.

It's important to note that the step value can also be a negative number. For example, using "for X = 50 to 1 by -1" would decrease the value of X from 50 to 49, 48, and so on.

Once the counter reaches the end of the specified range, the loop stops executing, and the program continues with statements that are not indented within the "for" loop.

In most programming languages, it is generally considered bad practice to modify the value of the counter variable from within the "for" loop statements, although it may be allowed in some languages. It's generally recommended to keep the counter variable separate from the loop control to maintain clarity and avoid confusion in the code.

The "while" loop statement

Similar to the "for" loop statement we learned about earlier, a "while" loop can also be used to repeat a set of statements. The "while" loop allows the execution of statements as long as a specified condition remains true. The "while" loop was introduced in version 5 of PineScript and is not available in previous versions.

You might wonder why the developers introduced the "while" loop when the "for" loop was already available. The "while" loop serves a different purpose and offers distinct advantages compared to the "for" loop. The primary difference lies in how the loop condition is evaluated and the control over the loop execution.

The syntax for a "while" loop is as follows:

```
While(condition)
    Statement1
    Statement1
.....
    Statements
```

The code statements to be repeated are written in the indented form below the while loop.

In the previous section, we calculated a simple moving average using "for loop"; below, we have again calculated SMA using a "while" loop.

INPUT LISTING IN.6.2 Calculating SMA using a while loop

```
// This source code is subject to the terms of the Mozilla Public License 2.0
// © achal

//@version=5
indicator("While Loop",overlay=true)
i=0
sum=0.0
while(i<7)
    sum:=sum+close[i]
    i:=i+1
myAvg7 = sum/7
plot(myAvg7)
```

Above is a script for calculating a simple moving average using a "while" loop. Try to identify differences with the "for" loop.

Fig IN.6.2: SMA calculated using a loop

ANALYSIS LISTING IN.6.2

In the given code, the variable "i" is used as a counter. Before entering the "while" loop, the initial value of "i" is set to zero. Within the loop, the value of "i" is incremented or modified in a way that eventually leads to the termination of the "while" loop. The remaining code inside the loop block is similar to the code used in a "for" loop.

Indeed, there are significant differences between the "while" loop and the "for" loop, and the two points you mentioned highlight some of these differences:

1. Counter Modification: In the "while" loop, you have the flexibility to modify the counter variable (in this case, "i") within the block of statements. This means that you can update the counter based on specific conditions or requirements as the loop progresses. In contrast, the "for" loop has a predefined counter that is automatically managed by the loop structure. The counter in a "for" loop is typically incremented automatically based on the specified range and step value, and you cannot modify it within the loop block.

2. User Management of the Counter: In a "while" loop, you have direct control over the counter variable. You are responsible for initializing the counter before the loop and managing its increment or modification within the loop block. On the other hand, in a "for" loop, the loop structure itself manages the counter. You only need to specify the range and step value, and the loop takes care of iterating over those values without requiring explicit counter management statements.

The introduction of the "while" loop alongside the "for" loop in programming languages serves specific purposes and offers additional flexibility in controlling the flow of execution. Here are the reasons why the "while" loop is required, even though we have the "for" loop:

Variable Condition: The "while" loop is designed for scenarios where the number of iterations or the exact condition for loop termination may not be known in advance. It allows you to define a condition that determines when the loop should continue or terminate. This makes the "while" loop more suitable for situations where you need to repeatedly execute a set of statements until a specific condition is met, regardless of the exact number of iterations.

Dynamic Control: Unlike the "for" loop, which operates based on a predefined range and step value, the "while" loop provides more dynamic control over the loop condition. You have the ability to change the condition within the loop block, allowing for adaptive decision-making and modifications to the loop behavior based on runtime conditions or external factors.

Event-Driven Execution: In event-driven programming or situations where the loop should continue until a certain event occurs, the "while" loop is often a better choice. It allows you to continuously check for the occurrence of an event or a specific condition, and as soon as that condition is satisfied, the loop can be terminated.

The "while" loop complements the "for" loop by offering a different approach to loop control. It provides flexibility in handling scenarios where the number of iterations is not known in advance or where dynamic control is required based on changing conditions. By using the appropriate loop construct, programmers can achieve greater control and efficiency in executing their code based on the specific requirements of their programs.

Summary

- Flowcharts are used to depict the flow of execution of calculation steps.
- A loop statement is used for repeating certain statements a specific number of times.
- A loop statement uses indentation for the identification of statements that are part of a loop
- A typical indentation has 4 spaces or a single tab before the beginning of a coding statement.
- If you want to change the value of an already defined variable, it cannot be done with a simple assignment ("="); it has to be done through a mutable variable assignment mark (":=")
- A for loop has three parts, a counter, a range providing lower and upper limit for the counter, and an incremental step.
- A counter can run in forward or reverse directions or can run in steps. By default, the step is one for 'for' statements.
- The "while" loops only work with pinescript version 5.
- For "while" loops, the condition should be made false from within the set of statements; otherwise, the code would keep executing forever.

Quiz

Q1. What would be the value of X in the second loop?

       For X = 3 to 100 step 3

a. 3	b. 6	c. 9	d. 12

Q2. What would be the value of Y after the execution of all the below statements?

       Y = 0
       For X = 9 to 3 step -3
       Y:= Y + X

a. 3	b. 6	c. 9	d. 18

Q3. What would be the value of Y after the execution of all the below statements?

       Y = 0
       For X = 9 to 3 step -3
          Y:= Y + X
          X:= 2

a. 3	b. 6	c. 9	d. error

Exercise

Q1. Write a program to calculate the average volume for the last 14 periods. Plot it below chart. (Hint: set overlay property to plot it below chart.)

Chapter -7: Control-flow: Branching

In the previous chapter, we discussed how control flow statements can alter the normal flow of program execution through decision-making, looping, and branching. These statements are essential for executing specific sets of statements conditionally. There are two primary types of control flow statements:

Looping Statements: Looping statements, such as the "for" loop and the "while" loop, allow us to repeat a specific set of statements multiple times. These loops are useful when we need to perform a task or execute a block of code iteratively until a certain condition is met. They provide a way to automate repetitive tasks and handle scenarios where the number of iterations is not known in advance.

Branching Statements: Branching statements, also known as conditional statements, enable us to make decisions and choose different paths of execution based on specific conditions. These statements include "if-else" statements, "switch" statements, and other conditional constructs. They allow us to perform different actions or execute different blocks of code based on the evaluation of conditions. Branching statements help in creating flexible and adaptive programs that can respond to varying conditions and inputs.

In the upcoming sections, we will explore examples that highlight the need for branching statements and demonstrate their applications in PineScript. By understanding these concepts, you will be able to create more dynamic and versatile scripts that can make decisions and respond to different scenarios based on specified conditions.

- The iff statement of version 4
- The ternary conditional Operator
- The "if….else…." statement

At certain points in a script, it becomes necessary to make decisions and choose different paths based on specific conditions. In PineScript, this can be achieved using conditional clauses. Conditional clauses consist of sets of script codes that are executed only if a particular condition, represented by an expression, evaluates to "true". Additionally, an optional part of the conditional clause can be executed when the condition evaluates to "false".

A common example of using conditional clauses is when coloring bars on a chart. For instance, if the close price is greater than the open price, the bar color can be set to green, indicating a positive price movement. On the other hand, if the close price is less than the open price, the bar color can be set to red, indicating a negative price movement. By using conditional clauses, the script can dynamically determine the appropriate color for each bar based on the condition being evaluated.

The iff statement in version 4

The "iff" statement has been removed from version 4; however, it is available in version 4 of pinescript. You may need to learn the "iff" statement to convert scripts written in version 4 by other coders into version 5. The "iff" statement gives a script the capability to make decisions. They execute code based on some condition. They select an action to perform based on the condition. This way, we make our script more flexible with more advanced behaviour. When something happens, like the candle is green or red or the volume is abnormally high, the indicator decides and takes action to handle the situation. The general format for the "iff" statement is as under:

Result_variable = iff(condition, then value1, else value2)

The data type of result_variable would depend on the "iff" statement. This can also be thought of as a conditional assignment to result_variable. If the condition is "true", the value immediately after the condition statement separated by a comma would be assigned to result_variable, and if the condition is "false", the second value after the condition statement is assigned to result_variable. Both variables' data types should be identical after the condition statement under the "iff" brackets. This "iff" statement is similar to the "if" statement that many of us may have already used in excel.

B2			✕	✓	ƒx	=IF(A1>B1,A1,B1)
	A	B	C	D	E	F
1	22	45				
2		45				

Fig: Use of "if" statement in excel

In the above example of excel, if A1 is > B1, the cell value would be the value stored in "A1"; else, it would be the value stored in B1. Instead of "if" in pine script, it is written as "iff". An example of a conditional assignment of colour constant to the color_const variable is given below:

color_const = iff(close > open, color.green, color.red)

If the close is more than open, the color_const variable would be green else red. An implementation example of "iff" is provided in IN.8. Note that this script is written in version 4 of pinescipt.

INPUT LISTING IN.7.1 Dynamic colouring of plot

```
1: // This source code is subject to the terms of the Mozilla Public License 2.0
2: // © Creating Trade Strategies & Backtesting Using PineScript - UDEMY
3: //@version=4
4: study("IN.8 Colouring of plot",overlay = true)
5: color_const = iff(close > open, color.green, color.red)
6: plot((high+low)/2,color=color_const)
```

OUTPUT LISTING IN.7.1

The plot in fig IN.7.1 is a plot of the mid-value of the bar. The colour of the plot changes depending on its 'close' value compared to the 'open' value. Also, note that we have used the keyword "study" instead of "indicator" as this is version 4 of pinescript. The keyword "study" has been replaced with the keyword "indicator" in version 5 of pinescript. The "iff" statement can only be used for the conditional assignment or the conditional execution of one statement. In case we have a set of statements that are required to be executed. The "iff" statement cannot be used.

Another point that should be remembered is that the datatype of result value on the condition being "true" and when "false" should be identical. It cannot be like, if true, the bar's colour would be green, and if false, the value would be 1000. This would become more clear once we have taken more examples.

Fig IN.7.1: Dynamic coloring of plot

ANALYSIS LISTING IN.7.1

It's understandable that the color distinction may not be visible in a black and white print. Executing the code in the PineScript editor will indeed provide a clearer understanding of the intended color changes. Visualization and interactive execution can greatly enhance the learning experience.

The ternary conditional operator

The ternary conditional operator is similar to the "iff" statement; however, it is considered efficient. All the "iff" statements written in version 4 should be edited suitably to a ternary operator to make them work under version 5 of pinescript. The topic should come under operator; however, this has been intentionally discussed hereunder branching as this is used to make decisions. The general format for the ternary conditional operator is as under:

result_variable = condition? result1: result2

In this format, the condition is evaluated. If the condition is true, the value assigned to result_variable is result1. If the condition is false, the value assigned to result_variable is result2. An example is as under, color_const = close > open? color.green:color.red

The condition close > open is evaluated. If the condition is true (i.e., the close price is greater than the open price), the color_const variable will be assigned the value color.green. If the condition is false, it will be assigned the value color.red.

The ternary conditional operator provides a concise way to assign values based on conditions, making your code more compact and readable. The values that the conditional operator can give back, i.e. result1 and result2, need to have the same data type. Here in the above example, both are constants for colour.

So, the code in version 4, as discussed in the "iff" statement section, can be converted to version 5 of pine script as under:

```
1: // This source code is subject to the terms of the Mozilla Public License 2.0
2: // © Creating Trade Strategies & Backtesting Using PineScript - UDEMY
3: //@version=5
4: indicator("IN.8 Colouring of plot",overlay = true)
5: color_const = close > open? color.green: color.red
6: plot((high+low)/2,color=color_const)
```

The "if....else..." statement

An "if" statement allows a script to make decisions based on certain conditions. It executes specific statements when the condition is true and skips those statements when the condition is false. It provides the flexibility to choose different actions based on different conditions, enhancing the script's behavior.

The "if" statement is an extension of the "iff" or ternary operator. While the ternary operator executes only one statement when true, the "if" statement allows multiple sets of statements to be executed.

The "if" statement evaluates a condition expression following the "if" keyword. If the condition is true, the statements within the corresponding block are executed. If the condition is false, an optional "else" block can be provided, and the statements within the "else" block are executed instead.

The "if" and "else" blocks are indented with equal leading spaces (one tab or 4 spaces) to clearly define the blocks of code. This indentation helps the system identify the scope of each block.

If there are multiple conditions to be checked, the "else if" statement can be used. It allows for multiple decision points and condition evaluations. The general format for using the "if else" statement is as follows:

If (condition)
    Statement 1
    Statement 2
else if (condition)
    Statement 4
    Statement 5
else
    Statement 6
    Statement 7

To use the "if" statement, the script version should be >= 2 of Pine Script language. The version of the script is defined in the first line of code, for example: //@version=5. From the 4th version onwards, Pine Script language has the "else if" functionality.

`INPUT` LISTING IN.7.2 Dynamic coloring of a plot using "if else".

```
01: // © Creating trade Strategies & Backtesting Using PineScript - UDEMY
02: //@version=5
03: indicator("Nested if-else statements",overlay = true)
04: color_value = color.blue
05: myplot = ta.sma(hl2,7)
06: if rsi(close,7) < 30
07:     color_value:= color.red
08: else if rsi(close,7) > 80
09:    color_value:= color.green
10: else
11:    color_value:= color.yellow
12:
13: plot(myplot,color=color_value,linewidth=3)
```

OUTPUT LISTING IN.7.2 Dynamic coloring of a plot using "if else"

Fig 7.2 Dynamic coloring of moving average

ANALYSIS LISTING IN.7.2

I have already discussed this above. In the case of a paperback book, the change of color would not be visible to the readers. You are requested to attempt the script in the pine script editor.

The script may give you a warning, though it would run. The warning would be to extract the call to ta.rsi from the ternary operator or from the scope. The meaning is to not run the ta.rsi functions from the local scope twice. The local scope will be covered in upcoming sections. However, the warning can be removed using the below code, wherein the RSI value can be stored in the "myRSI" variable and used in the conditional operator.

```
// © Creating trade Strategies & Backtesting Using PineScript – UDEMY
//@version=5
indicator("Nested if-else statements",overlay = true)
color_value = color.blue
myplot = ta.sma(hl2,7)
myRSI = ta.rsi(close,7)
if myRSI < 30
    color_value:= color.red
else if myRSI > 80
    color_value:= color.green
else
    color_value:= color.yellow
plot(myplot,color=color_value,linewidth=3)
```

Summary

- A branch code of your script allows choosing between a set of blocks of statements. Code only executes if a particular expression (the condition) is 'true'.
- The "iff" statement is not supported in version 5
- The "iff" statement is similar to excel's if statement and is used for the conditional assignment or execution of one statement.
- The "iff" statement can only be used for the conditional assignment or the conditional execution of one statement.
- The ternary conditional operator(?) is similar to the "iff" statement. However, it is considered efficient. A ternary conditional operator is also used for conditional assignment.
- Unlike the "iff" statement, the "if....else..." statement can execute multiple statement lines.
- The "if" and "else" blocks are indented, i.e. have equal leading space before the start of the line so the system can identify these block statements.
- Version 4 onwards of pinescript provides the option to use another if after else in the format "else if"

Quiz

Q1. What would be the value of result_variable

A = 1.1

B = 2

result_variable = 4

result_variable:= A>B?A:B

a.	1.1	c. 4
b.	2	d. error

Q.2 What would be the value of result_variable

A = 1.1

B = 2.0

result_variable = 4.0

result_variable:= iff(A>B,A,B)

a.	1.1	c. 4
b.	2	d. error

Q.3 What would be the value of result_variable

A = 1.1

B = 2.0

if A> B

      result_variable = 100

else if A > 4

      result_variable = 200

else

      result_variable = 300

a.	100	c. 300
b.	200	d. error

Exercise

Q.1 Write IN.8 script using the "iff" statement only.

Q.2 Write IN.7 "Dynamic colouring of plot" using conditional operator statement (?).

Chapter -8: Functions

As discussed in earlier lessons, the Pine Script language focuses on trading and allows for the coding of indicators and strategies. Every language or package has a specific focus area. MATLAB is used for mathematical modeling, whereas ASP.NET, PERL, etc., are used for web designing. Every language has built-in code that its users can reuse.

Built-in Functions in PineScript

Pine Script is a programming language specifically designed for trading purposes. It enables users to write code for creating indicators and strategies that help in analyzing financial markets. Pine Script is tailored for trading-related tasks. Pine Script provides a range of pre-built functions, indicators, and tools that traders can utilize in their code, making it easier to implement common trading concepts and perform various calculations and analyses specific to the financial markets.

In march 2020, new common indicators were added to pinescript. The following are major indicator functions available in Pinescript:

- cmo - Chande Momentum Oscillator
- mfi - Money Flow Index
- bb - Bollinger Bands
- bbw - Bollinger Bands Width
- kc - Keltner Channels
- kcw - Keltner Channels Width
- dmi - DMI/ADX
- wpr - Wouldiams % R
- hma - Hull Moving Average
- supertrend – SuperTrend

Some other indicators already available in pinescript before March 2020 are
- cog – center of gravity
- rsi – relative strength index
- stoch - stochastic indicator
- sar – Parabolic stop and reverse

We will be discussing implementation and coding for some of them so that you can use them effectively in your coding and strategies.

Chande Momentum Oscillator

Tushar Chande introduced the Chande Momentum Oscillator in 1994. This oscillator is calculated by finding the difference between recent gains and losses. The gains and losses are then averaged by summing all price movements.

In Pine Script, you don't need to worry about the detailed calculations, as the language provides a built-in function called "cmo" to calculate the Chande Momentum Oscillator. You simply need to provide the 'close' values and specify the period for which you want to calculate the oscillator, and the result will be calculated using the "cmo" function.

The syntax for implementation of Chande Momentum Oscillator is

```
cmo_value = ta.cmo (series, length)
```

The above syntax is similar to simple moving average syntax; you provide series 'close' values and 7 periods or 14 periods as length for calculating Chande Momentum Oscillator.

As the name suggests, it is an oscillator, and therefore it is plotted below the price chart. You have to make overlay=false for this indicator. A simple code for the implementation is provided below for ready reference.

INPUT LISTING IN.8.1 Implementing Chande Momentum Oscillator

```
//@version=5
indicator("CMO Example",overlay=false)
cmo_value = ta.cmo(close, 14)
plot(cmo_value)
```

OUTPUT LISTING IN.8.1 Implementing Chande Momentum Oscillator

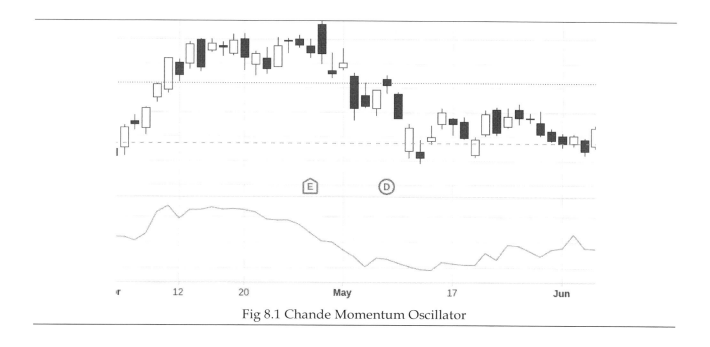

Fig 8.1 Chande Momentum Oscillator

Now, the question arises, how can we use CMO for trading or strategy purposes? In my experience, all oscillators like RSI work in a similar fashion. Here are some common approaches you can consider:

Divergence: Look for divergences between the price and the CMO. Divergence occurs when the price and the CMO move in opposite directions. Bullish divergence happens when the price makes lower lows while the CMO makes higher lows, indicating potential buying opportunities. Conversely, bearish divergence occurs when the price makes higher highs while the CMO makes lower highs, suggesting potential selling opportunities.

Overbought and Oversold Levels: As you mentioned, the CMO values range from -100 to 100. You can consider selling when the CMO value is near or above a specific threshold (e.g., 50), indicating an overbought condition. Similarly, you may consider buying when the CMO value is near or below a certain threshold (e.g., -50), suggesting an oversold condition. However, it's important to note that these threshold levels should be validated based on historical price behavior and market conditions.

Moving Average Crossovers: Calculate a moving average of the CMO values for a smaller period, known as the signal line. Look for crossovers between the CMO values and the signal line. When the CMO crosses above the signal line, it could signal a potential bullish trend or buying opportunity. Conversely, when the CMO crosses below the signal line, it may indicate a potential bearish trend or selling opportunity. Experiment with different periods for the signal line to find the one that works best for your trading strategy.

A sample code for the implementing signal line is provided below:

```
//@version=5
indicator("CMO Example",overlay=false)
cmo_value1 = ta.sma(ta.cmo(close, 14),3)
signal = ta.sma(ta.cmo(close,14),7)
plot(cmo_value1)
plot(signal)
```

I have calculated the moving average of the Chande Momentum Oscillator (CMO) for 3 periods to smooth out the curve of the CMO and filter out noise. Additionally, I have used a 7-day period for the CMO signal line. These specific values for smoothing and signal line period can be adjusted based on your trading preferences and the specific market conditions you are analyzing.

The concept of using a crossover between an oscillator and a signal line can be applied to various other momentum indicators such as the Directional Movement Index (DMI), Williams %R (WPR), Money Flow Index (MFI), Relative Strength Index (RSI), and more. By adjusting the smoothing periods and signal line periods for each specific indicator, you can customize and fine-tune your trading strategy to better suit your trading style and market conditions.

Bollinger Bands

The Bollinger Bands indicator is commonly used on price charts. When using this indicator, the "overlay" parameter is set to true, which allows the bands to be plotted directly on the price chart. The Bollinger Bands consist of three lines: the upper band line, the lower band line, and the middle line.

The middle line represents the moving average of the price data. The upper band line is created by adding a certain number of standard deviations to the moving average, while the lower band line is created by subtracting the same number of standard deviations from the moving average.

The standard deviation is a statistical measure of volatility, and it helps determine the width of the Bollinger Bands. When price volatility increases, the bands expand, and when volatility decreases, the bands contract.

In PineScript, you don't need to calculate all these values manually. The built-in function "bb" is available for calculating the Bollinger Bands. By providing the necessary inputs, such as the source data (e.g., close price), length, and number of standard deviations, you can easily plot the Bollinger Bands on the chart without the need for manual calculations. The syntax for implementing the Bollinger band is shown below:

```
[middle_value, upper_band_value, lower_band_value] = ta.bb(series, length, stdev)
```

When using the ta.bb function in PineScript, the default values for the parameters are typically set to close for the series, 20 for the length, and 2 for the standard deviation.

The ta.bb function generates three outputs, representing the middle value, upper band value, and lower band value of the Bollinger Bands. These outputs are in the order of middle, upper, and lower values.

You can use these output values accordingly based on your trading or analysis strategy. For example, you might compare the price with the upper band value to identify potential overbought conditions, or compare the price with the lower band value to identify potential oversold conditions. The middle value can provide an indication of the current price trend or act as a reference level.

A simple implementation of the Bollinger band in pinescript is provided below:

INPUT LISTING IN.8.2 Implementing Bollinger Bands

```
//@version=5
indicator("BB example",overlay=true)
[middle_value,upper_value,lower_value]=ta.bb(close, 20,2)
plot(middle_value)
plot(upper_value,color=color.green)
plot(lower_value,color=color.green)
```

OUTPUT LISTING IN.8.2 Bollinger Bands

Fig IN.8.2 Bollinger Band

The output generated by the Bollinger band is shown above. The output generated by the Bollinger Bands indicator provides valuable information for trading decisions. The bands can be effectively used when prices cross either the upper or lower band lines.

The underlying logic behind this strategy is based on the assumption that price distribution follows a normal distribution. When the price crosses the upper band line, which is typically two standard deviations away from the middle line, there is a 95% probability that the price will revert back to the mean, represented by the middle line. Similarly, if the price crosses the lower band line, the same principle applies.

In situations where the price crosses three standard deviations, the probabilistic chances of price returning to the mean increase to 99.7%. This provides a stronger indication for potential price reversals.

Additionally, Bollinger Bands also reflect volatility. When the bands contract, it suggests that price volatility is low, and there is a higher likelihood of an impending price breakout or significant price movement. These indicators should be combined with other indicators to filter out false signals.

Keltner Channels

Keltner Channels, like Bollinger Bands, are a popular technical indicator used for analyzing price volatility. In PineScript, the "kc" function is available to calculate Keltner Channels, providing three output values: the middle line, upper band, and lower band.

The calculation of Keltner Channels differs from Bollinger Bands in terms of the volatility measure used. Instead of standard deviation, Keltner Channels utilize the Average True Range (ATR) to determine the width of the bands. ATR is known for capturing price volatility more effectively, resulting in smoother bands compared to Bollinger Bands.

The syntax for using Keltner Channels in PineScript is as follows:

```
[middle_value, upper_band_value, lower_band_value] = ta.kc(series, length, multiplier for ATR)
```

The default values of close for series, 20 for length and 2 for multiplier for ATR can be used.

The trading strategies are similar to Bollinger band as Keltner Channel have been developed on Bollinger band's theory. Try implementing Keltner Channels yourself by taking reference from code of Bollinger band.

Center of Gravity

The "Center of Gravity" indicator, developed by John Ehlers, is known for its potential in identifying turning points in price movements. While some claims suggest zero lag, it is important to note that achieving true zero lag is challenging in technical analysis. However, compared to other indicators, the Center of Gravity indicator exhibits relatively less lag.

One advantage of the Center of Gravity indicator is its smoothness, which makes it easier to implement and interpret. It provides a visual representation of the balance between bullish and bearish forces in the market, helping traders identify potential reversal points.

It is worth mentioning that the effectiveness of the Center of Gravity indicator can vary depending on market conditions and the timeframe being analyzed. Traders often combine it with other indicators or trading strategies to enhance its accuracy and effectiveness. The syntax for the cog indicator is as under:

```
cog_value = ta.cog(source, length)
```

The implementation of the Center of Gravity (COG) indicator is indeed simple and straightforward. It requires two inputs and produce one outpur, similar to the Simple Moving Average (SMA) indicator.

To use the COG indicator, you can input the "close" value as the source for calculation. Additionally, you can set the length or lookback period to 10, which determines the number of previous periods considered in the calculation.

To create a signal line, you can calculate the SMA of the COG indicator for a specific number of days, such as 3 days. This signal line can provide additional insights and help identify potential entry or exit points in your trading strategy.

By combining the COG indicator with a signal line, you can gain a better understanding of the price movement and potential reversals in the market. A sample code is presented below:

INPUT LISTING IN.8.3 Implementing Center of Gravity

```
//@version=5
indicator("COG example",overlay=false)
cog_value=ta.cog(close, 10)
signal_value = ta.sma(ta.cog(close,10),3)
plot(cog_value,color=color.green)
plot(signal_value,color=color.blue)
```

The output generated by the COG indicator is displayed below the price chart in output section. The indicator is known for its smoothness, which helps in clearly visualizing the crossovers without excessive noise or false signals. This characteristic makes it easier to identify potential trend changes based on the indicator's behavior.

One of the valuable applications of the COG indicator is its ability to detect divergences between the price and the indicator itself. Divergence occurs when the price moves in one direction while the indicator moves in the opposite direction. This can indicate a potential reversal or change in the underlying trend.

By observing and analyzing the divergence between the price and the COG indicator, traders can gain insights into possible trend shifts and make informed trading decisions. Divergence between the price and the COG indicator occurs when they move in opposite directions. In other words, the price may be showing one trend while the COG indicator is showing a different trend. This can be a potential signal of a trend reversal or change in the market.

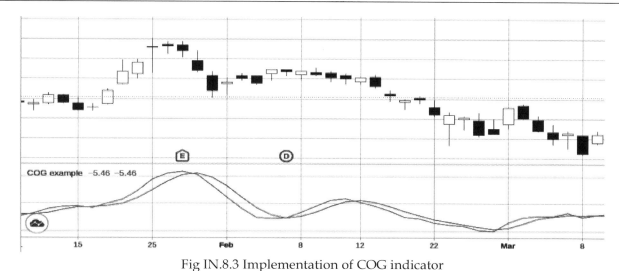

Fig IN.8.3 Implementation of COG indicator

Other indicators, along with COG, can filter trade signals. The literature on COG suggests that it should be used in a range-bound market and not in trending markets. An ADX can be added to the chart wherein COG can be traded if a value is less than 25.

Fig IN.8.4 Trading Opportunities using COG with ADX

The ADX is a trend strength indicator that measures the strength of a trend, whether it's an uptrend or a downtrend. By adding the ADX to the chart and checking if its value is less than 25, you can identify a range-bound market condition. In a range-bound market, where the ADX value is below 25, the COG indicator can be used to identify potential turning points or reversals within the established range.

Here is the code used to generate the trade opportunities based on the crossover and crossunder of the COG indicator with the signal lines, while considering the ADX value below 25. You can observe that most of the trades are on the winning side.

Some of the code lines may not be clear to you at this point, but you will gain a better understanding as you progress through this book.

```
//@version=5
indicator("COG example",overlay=true)
cog_value= ta.cog(close, 10)
signal_value = ta.sma(ta.cog(close,10),3)


adxlen = input(14, title="ADX Smoothing")
dilen = input(14, title="DI Length")
dirmov(len) =>
        up = ta.change(high)
        down = -ta.change(low)
        plusDM = na(up)? na: (up > down and up > 0? up: 0)
        minusDM = na(down)? na: (down > up and down > 0? down: 0)
        truerange = ta.rma(ta.tr, len)
        plus = fixnan(100 * ta.rma(plusDM, len) / truerange)
        minus = fixnan(100 * ta.rma(minusDM, len) / truerange)
        [plus, minus]
adx(dilen, adxlen) =>
        [plus, minus] = dirmov(dilen)
        sum = plus + minus
        adx = 100 * ta.rma(math.abs(plus - minus) / (sum == 0? 1: sum), adxlen)
sig = adx(dilen, adxlen)

plotshape(ta.crossover(cog_value,signal_value) and sig<25, location = location.belowbar, color=
  color.green)
plotshape(ta.crossunder(cog_value,signal_value)  and  sig<25,  location=  location.abovebar,
color=
```

```
color.red)
```

You can utilize the above code to verify trade signals on other scripts and customize it by adding additional filters to suit your specific requirements. By experimenting and incorporating your own parameters, you can refine the trading strategy and adapt it to different market conditions. Remember to thoroughly test any modifications before implementing them in live trading.

Users of the PineScript language often make use of built-in functions and user-defined functions in their code. Functions allow for the reuse of code, making the coding process faster and more convenient. Instead of writing the same code repeatedly, functions encapsulate a set of instructions that can be called and executed whenever needed. There are two types of functions in PineScript:

Built-in Functions: These functions are pre-defined in PineScript and provide various functionalities to perform calculations, access data, and generate indicators. Examples of built-in functions include sma(), rsi(), ema(), close, etc. These functions are ready to use and don't require additional coding.

User-defined Functions: Users can create their own functions in PineScript to perform specific tasks or calculations that are not available as built-in functions. User-defined functions are written by the user and can be customized to suit their specific needs. These functions can be reused throughout the script, improving code organization and readability. The following sections discuss functions in PineScript:

- The need for user-defined functions
- Understanding a function
- Defining Custom Functions in PineScript
    - Simple Single line Function
    - Multi-line function with a single return
    - Multiline function with Multiple Return
- Scope of variable
    - Function without argument with a return value

We have already studied built-in functions such as simple moving averages, relative strength index, exponential moving average, and so on. All of these codes are referred to as functions because they take specific inputs and provide results. For example, when calculating the RSI, you need to specify the length of the lookback period and indicate the source (close or open value) on which the calculation should be performed. The inputs provided to a function are called arguments of the function. In technical terms, the arguments are enclosed in parentheses after the function's name, separated by commas, and the output is stored in the designated variable on the left-hand side.

outputResult = functionName(argument1, argument2, argument3)

The need for user-defined functions

You may find it beneficial to reuse a set of code multiple times within a script or make your code modular and shareable with other coders by defining functions. PineScript allows you to define your own functions, which simplifies your code and makes it more efficient.

In LISTING IN.6, we saw an example of calculating a simple moving average without using a built-in function. We observed that the code without using a built-in function was lengthy. If we were to calculate a crossover between two moving averages, we would have to repeat the entire procedure. This is where built-in functions come in handy. However, there are many indicators or ideas that are not readily available as built-in functions. In such cases, you can create your own functions to implement these indicators or ideas. By using functions, you can neatly incorporate them into your program and reuse them multiple times without having to rewrite the original code.

Understanding a function

The general format for a function is as under:

outputResult = functionName(argument1, argument2, argument3)

The function's input is written in brackets following the function's name. These inputs are used in the calculation or execution of functional block statements. For instance, in a simple moving average function, the inputs are 'close' and the lookback period, which serves as the length. The result produced by such functions is stored in the variable "outputResult" on the left-hand side of the assignment operator.

Not all functions necessarily have an output; therefore, the output variable is optional and may not be needed. For example, in a plot function, the input consists of a series to be plotted, the line color, width, etc. However, the output is simply the line displayed and not a result that needs to be stored. Consequently, in these types of functions, the output variable may be absent.

While most functions return a single result, there could be cases where multiple outputs or results are generated.In such cases, the function is implemented in the manner suggested below:

[Result1, Result2] = functionName(Argument1, Argument2.......)

The multiple results obtained from a function are stored in the result variables separated by a comma on the left-hand side of the assignment operator. It is essential to note that the order of the result variables must match the order of the output produced by the function. For instance, consider the "ta.bb" function for the Bollinger band indicator. In the upcoming sections, we will create custom functions and use specific examples to demonstrate their applications and functionality.

Defining Custom Functions in Script

1.   **Simple Single line Function**
     Simple functions can often be written in one line. An example of the single-line function is provided below:

```
myHL2(highSeries,lowSeries) => (highSeries+lowSeries)/2
```

In the given example, the "=>" symbol indeed indicates the declaration of a function, where the left side specifies the function's name along with its input arguments, and it denotes that the user is defining a function.

So, "myHL2" is the name of the function, and its inputs are 'high' and 'low'. The result that this function produces is a single return value, which is calculated as (high + low) / 2.

B.   **Multiline function with Single Return**
     Let's see an example of a simple moving average calculation turned into a function.

```
mySMA(inputSeries,inputLength) =>
```

```
sum = 0.0
for counter = 0 to inputLength-1
    sum:= sum + inputSeries[counter]
myOutput = sum/inputLength
myOutput
```

The function "mySMA" can take two inputs: 1) "inputSeries" and 2) "inputLength". You can provide any series as input to calculate the SMA by using the following format:

resultValue = mySMA(high, 7)

This will calculate the moving average for seven periods of the "high" series and store the result in the "resultValue" variable.

Inside the function, the variable "inputSeries" takes the value of 'high', and "inputLength" takes the value 7. The calculation is performed based on these input values, and the result is stored in the "myOutput" variable.

The final line of the function, which contains only one variable "myOutput," signifies that this is the result value that should be returned. When this function is executed, the result is stored in the "resultValue" variable.

Additionally, the code indentation is worth noting. The code block of a function has indentation (4 spaces or one tab), and the loop inside the function requires further indentation. To maintain clarity, the entire code block of the function is indented uniformly, while the loop inside the function has been indented with extra space (8 spaces or 2 tabs) for identification. "LISTING IN.8.4" provides the complete code for plotting the result obtained from "mySMA."

INPUT LISTING IN.8.4 Plotting mySMA function

```
03: //@version=5
04: indicator("Plotting mySMA function",overlay = true)
05: mySMA(inputSeries,inputLength) =>
06:     sum = 0.0
07:     for counter = 0 to inputLength-1
```

```
08:        sum:= sum + inputSeries[counter]
09:
10:    myOutput = sum/inputLength
11:    myOutput
12: resultValue = mySMA(close,7)
13: plot(resultValue,color=color.red,linewidth=2)
```

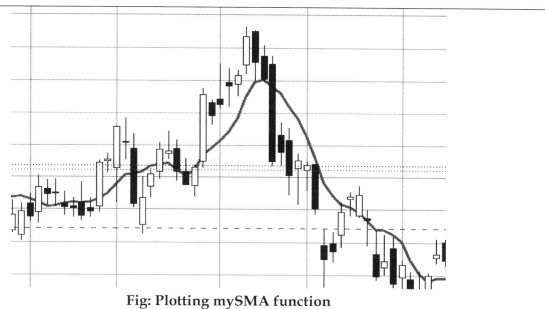

Fig: Plotting mySMA function

The plot in fig IN.8.4 is produced by a custom function created by us. Here it is plotting SMA of close calculated basis last 7 periods.

ANALYSIS LISTING IN.8.4

In line 5, the function "mySMA" has been defined by specifying its name followed by the inputs it can take, which are written inside parentheses and separated by commas. The names of the inputs can be anything; they act as variables and store the actual input values when the function is called. Creating a function to perform a calculation is known as "calling a function". The function is called on line 12.

The "=>" symbol is used to declare a function and should not be confused with the greater than or equal to sign (">="). In Pine Script, the greater than or equal to sign is denoted as ">=".

Line 6 initializes a new variable called "sum" and sets it equal to 0.0 instead of just 0. This makes the "sum" variable a float, capable of storing numbers with their decimal parts, rather than an integer.

Line 7 contains a loop statement "for counter = 0 to inputLength-1". The variable "inputLength" is subtracted by 1 because the counting starts from 0 to include the current bar. If the loop counter were to start from 1 to 7, it would still calculate the 7-day moving average, but the current bar would not be part of the calculated average; technically, it would be a moving average with an offset of -1, meaning it is shifted by 1 bar.

Lines 8 to 11 are part of the function "mySMA"; therefore, all these lines require indentation. Furthermore, only line 8 is part of the "for" loop, so it requires further indentation. Line 8 calculates the cumulative sum of "inputSeries". Line 10 calculates the moving average and stores it in "myOutput". Line 11 consists of only the variable "myOutput" and serves as the last line of the function, instructing the system to return this variable as the result.

Line 13 is used to plot the "myOutput" variable. The plot function has been discussed in detail in previous lessons.

C. **Multiline function with Multiple Return**
   The multiple return function is declared in the following format:
   myFunctionName(A, B) =>
         A = A+B
         B = A-B
         [A, B]

The values returned by the function are written in square brackets on the last line and separated by a comma. When these are called, i.e. they are required to compute in your program, they can be called in the format provided below.

[X, Y]= myFunctionName(A, B)

Below is an example of a function:
```
myFunctionName(O,H,L,C) =>
            myHL2 = (H+L)/2
            myHLC3 = (H+L+C)/3
            myOHLC4 = (H+L+C+O)/4
            [myHL2,myHLC3,myOHLC4]
```

The call for the function would look like this:

[myHL2,myHLC3,myOHLC4] = myFunctionName(open,high,low,close)

O, H, L, and C variables in the function take the open, high, low, and close, respectively and would do the calculation per the instructions. The result is returned from the last line of function and stored in the same order on the left side variables. The variable names on the left side of the functions could be different from the name of the return variables, like

[valHL2,valHLC3,valOHLC4] = myFunctionName(open,high,low,close)

You must ensure that the order of variables on the left side of a function is the same as that of return variables.

Scope of Variables

Global variables are defined at the beginning of the script and are not indented within any specific code block. These global variables can be accessed from any part of the script.

Built-in variables are also considered global variables, meaning they can be accessed from any part of the script. On the other hand, variables defined inside a function are referred to as local variables because they exist only within the scope of that function and cannot be accessed outside of its code block.

Function without argument with a return value

It is not necessary to pass global variables as arguments to functions because they can be accessed from any part of the script. The function "myHL2" calculates the midpoint of the bar, and its arguments will always be the built-in variables "high" and "low". Hence, there is no need to provide global variables as arguments to the function.

The function myHL2(highSeries,lowSeries)=> (highSeries+lowSeries)/2 can thus be rewritten as:

myHL2() =>(high+low)/2

The function does not have an argument, i.e. input value. However, this would have the same result.

Example Code:

```
//@version=5
indicator("Plotting mySMA of HL2 function",overlay = true)
myHL2() => (high+low)/2
myHL2result = myHL2()
mySMA(inputSeries,inputLength) =>
    sum = 0.0
    for counter = 0 to inputLength-1
        sum:= sum + inputSeries[counter]

    myOutput = sum/inputLength
    myOutput
resultValue = mySMA(myHL2result,7)
plot(resultValue,color=color.red,linewidth=2)
```

Library

In version 5 of Pine Script, a new feature called "library" has been introduced, which allows you to create reusable code in the form of functions. With this feature, you can export functions from a file that is already saved and import them into your current script without the need to copy the entire function's code.

Using libraries in Pine Script helps organize your code better, reduces the need for repeating code, and makes your scripts more maintainable and readable.

Let's demonstrate this feature with an example. Suppose we want to create a new function to calculate the Simple Moving Average (SMA), which takes only the "length" as input and uses the "close" as the data source.

Exporting function from a library

The library file can be created using the open tab under pinescript editor and clicking on the "new blank library" tab.

```
01: //@version=5
02:
03: library("mySMA")
04:
05: export mySMA(int x) =>
06:     ta.sma(close,x)
```

In the above code, line 1 specifies the version of PineScript as version 5. Line 3 declares that this file is a "library" and not an "indicator". The library arguments, such as the title and overlay, can be added to modify the behavior of the library.

The library can be coded in PineScript as demonstrated in previous sections. You can export functions from the library to other scripts by creating functions under the library script with the "export" keyword before the function name.

At line 5, the function "mySMA" has been declared to take only one input, which is an integer. The function returns the Simple Moving Average (SMA) for the 'x' period calculated on the 'close' price. The 'close' is an in-built variable that can be accessed from any part of the code; hence, it is not specified as another input. The new SMA function in this example only requires the length as an input because it calculates the SMA based on the 'close' value of the bar.

After creating the library file, you can save it in your TradingView cloud storage space. Before using this script in another file, you must publish it. You can publish it "privately", meaning only you or anyone with the link can import the library. Alternatively, you can choose to publish the script "publicly", allowing anyone from the PineScript community to search and use your script.

Once you publish the code, you get a path for importing the script code. This link would be in the format:

Username/name of the library/ version of the code

For example, if I save and publish the above code with the library title as "mySMA" and suppose my username is "achal", the library link for accessing the exported function is:

> "achal/mySMA/1"

Importing function from the library

Once you've published your library script as either a public or private script, you'll be able to access the functions from the library script in another script using the "import" keyword. You should use the "import" keyword along with the path to the library to import all functions.

```
01: //@version=5
02: indicator("test lib")
03: import achal/mySMA/1 as s
04: plot(s.mySMA(7))
05: plot(s.mySMA(14))
```

Another crucial point to note is that all functions imported from a library script must be stored in an alias namespace. You can specify this alias after the path name using the "as" keyword. Below is the syntax for importing functions from the library and making them available through an "alias":

```
import [username/library name/version] as [alias name]
```

The alias name can be thought of as a container that holds information for all the functions imported from the library, also referred to as a "namespace". For instance, "ta" serves as a namespace for all the technical indicator functions, while "math" functions form a namespace for math-related operations in Pine Script. In the example provided, on line 3, the import keyword is utilized to bring in a library file named "mySMA," as created in the previous section. All functions within the library file are stored in the namespace "s."

Using a dot operator allows access to functions within the namespace. In simpler terms, any functions stored in the namespace can be accessed using a dot operator. For instance, the mySMA function created in the previous section can be accessed using "s.mySMA", where "s" represents the namespace for all functions obtained from the imported library file.

Summary

- A function is a block of reusable code that can be employed multiple times within your script. It enhances script clarity and readability while facilitating other coders in recognizing and reusing your functions.
- The "=>" symbol is used to declare functions and should not be mistaken for the greater-than or equal-to sign, which is represented as ">=" in Pine Script.

- Functions may consist of a single line or multiple lines, with or without arguments, and may return a single result, multiple results, or no result.
- Function inputs are enclosed within brackets following the function name and are separated by commas.
- Results of a function are stored in variables on the left-hand side of the assignment operator.
- Variables defined within a function are inaccessible outside of the function.
- Global variables and built-in variables are accessible from any part of the script.

Quiz

Q1. What would be the value of myResult after execution of the following code if ta.sma(close,7) is greater than ta. sma(close,14):

```
myResult = ta.sma(close,7) > ta.sma(close,14)? true: false
```

Q2. What would be the value of myResult after execution of the following code, if ta.sma(close,7) is greater than ta.sma(close,14):

```
myCrossover() => ta.sma(close,7) > ta.sma(close,14)? true: false
myResult = myCrossover()
```

Q3. What would be the value of myResult after execution of the following code, if ta.sma(close,7) is greater than ta.sma(close,14):

```
myCrossover() =>
        If (ta.sma(close,7) > ta.sma(close,14))
                myReturn =  true
        else
                myReturn = false
        myReturn
myResult = myCrossover()
```

Q4. What would be the value of myResult after execution of the following code, if myRSI value is 21

```
Crossing = true
myRSI = ta.rsi(close, 14)
myBuy(Crossover,myRSI)=>
```

```
        If (Crossover == false)
                myDecision = false
        else if (myrsi < 25)
                myDecision = true
        myDecision
myResult = myBuy(Crossing,myRSI)
```

Exercise

Q1. Write a function for finding the lowest of three numbers. Input would be three variables, and output should be the lowest of the three variables.

Chapter-09: Examples using Functions

In the previous lesson, you learned about functions and their usefulness in programming. You've discovered how convenient it is to reuse blocks of code through functions. In this lesson, we'll delve into some examples that demonstrate the practical application of functions.

ZigZag Indicator

The Zig Zag indicator draws lines that connect the highest and lowest points on a chart whenever prices reverse. When a green candle is succeeded by a red candle, or vice versa, the highest or lowest points of the last two bars are identified and utilized for generating the Zig Zag indicator. This indicator aids in identifying price trends by filtering out price fluctuations and aiming to reveal clear changes in trend direction. Below is the code for the Zig Zag indicator.

ZigZag Indicator code in Version 2
Below is the code for the zigzag indicator. The code is relatively straightforward to comprehend. It includes a new built-in function, nz(). Additionally, a built-in value 'na' is utilized within the code. The term 'na', as implied, stands for "no value". A detailed explanation of the code is provided below for better understanding:

`INPUT` LISTING IN.10 ZigZag Indicator in Version 2

```
//This source code is subject to the terms of the Mozilla Public License 2.0
// teach yourself trade strategies in PineScript

//@version=2
study(title='Example ZigZag',overlay=true)
zigzag() =>
        _isUp = close >=open
        _isDown = close <= open
        _direction = _isUp[1] and _isDown? -1:_isDown[1] and _isUp? 1:nz(_direction[1])
        _zigzag = _isUp[1] and _isDown and _direction[1] != -1?
         highest(2): _isDown[1] and _isUp and _direction[1] != 1? lowest(2): na

sz = zigzag()
plot(sz,title='zigzag',color=blue,linewidth=2)
```

OUTPUT LISTING IN.10

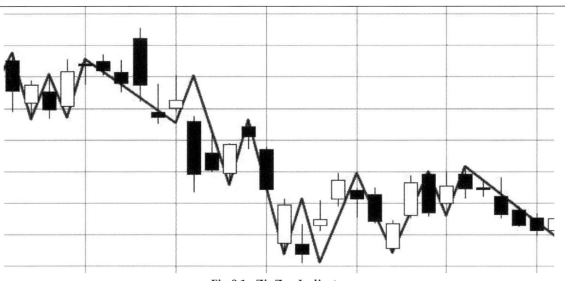

Fig 9.1 : ZigZag Indicator

ANALYSIS LISTING IN.10

Upon initial inspection, it's evident that the code is composed in version 2. Versions 2 and 5 exhibit disparities. Familiarizing oneself with both versions is crucial for assimilating code from other users and incorporating it into projects. To facilitate understanding of the code's evolution, the same script is also provided in version 5, allowing for a comparative study of the differences between these two versions.

Line 6 defines the function's name, i.e. zigzag; it takes no arguments, so we have blank brackets '()'. Function declaration sign "=>" instructs the system to consider zigzag a function.

The _isUP and _isDown are boolean variables. They store values in true and false depending on the condition. If a bar is upbar, _isUP is 'true', and if a bar is downbar, _isDown is true; else, they would be false.

Line 9 has two conditional operators clubbed with each other in "if….else" style. The first part of the first conditional operator is:

 _direction = _isUp[1] and _isDown? -1: condition to be executed on being false

The _direction is an integer variable. If the last bar is upbar and the current bar is down bar, it is a change of direction in a downward direction, and the -1 value gets stored in the _direction variable. In the case of false, another conditional operator gets triggered.

_isDown[1] and _isUp? 1: nz(_direction[1])

If the last bar is a down bar and the current bar is an up bar, it is again a change of direction in the upward direction, and 1 value gets stored in the _direction variable. If the condition is false, the _direction variable equals nz(_direction[1]). In simpler terms, the _direction variable stores the _direction value of the previous bar. Here a new inbuilt value, 'nz', has been used. The nz is a "filler"; it fills na values of a series with zeros. If the previous _direction variable has no value, i.e. 'na', it makes it zero.

If the current bar is in a rising trend, i.e. the current bar is up bar, and the previous bar was also upbar, it would have _direction value as 1, and similarly, in a downward trend _direction would have -1 values. At the point of change in direction, the values of two consecutive bars would be -1,1, indicating a change to the upward direction or 1,-1, signifying a change to the downward direction.

Line 10 & 11 again has two consecutive conditional operators. The code line has since become long; it continued on line 11. To do this, you have to use indentation. However, do not do standard indentation of one tab or 4 spaces. Here I have used 2 spaces. The first part of the first conditional operator is

_zigzag = _isUp[1] and _isDown and _direction[1] != -1? highest(2): condition to be executed on being false

If the last bar is upbar and the current bar is down the bar, and the direction is not downward, _zigzag value would be the highest of the last two bars. In case this condition is false, the following conditional operator is triggered

_zigzag = _isDown[1] and _isUp   and _direction[1] != 1? lowest(2): na

If the last bar is a down bar and the current bar is upbar and the direction is not upward, the value of the _zigzag variable would be the lowest value of the last two bars. If these conditions are not satisfied, the value of _zigzag would be 'na', i.e. nothing.

For clarity, we take an example:

Open	High	low	Close	_isUP	_isDown	_direction	_zigzag

34.1	34.6	34.1	34.5	True	False	Na	Na
34.4	34.8	34.3	34.8	True	False	Na	Na
34.9	35.0	34.4	34.5	False	True	-1	35.0
34.4	34.5	33.9	34.2	False	True	-1	na
34.1	34.8	34.1	34.6	True	False	1	33.9
34.7	35.1	34.5	35.0	True	False	1	na

Zigzag Indicator in version 5

At the time of writing this book, the latest version of Pine Script is 5. While the code provided in Pine Script version 2, as discussed earlier, is straightforward to understand and utilize, the developers of Pine Script have made certain changes to enhance system efficiency and address technicalities. Below is version 5 of the same script we discussed earlier. Attempting to compile the version 2 script on version 5 of Pine Script would result in errors and prevent execution.

As new versions of Pine Script emerge, this book will remain relevant for an extended period. New versions introduce additional capabilities to the script while retaining existing functionalities. Furthermore, newer versions maintain backward compatibility to accommodate existing users as they transition to the new version.

`INPUT` LISTING IN.11 ZigZag Indicator in Version 5

```
//@version=5
indicator(title='Example ZigZag',overlay=true)
zigzag() =>
        _isUp = close >=open
        _isDown = close <= open
        _direction=0
        _direction:= _isUp[1] and _isDown? -1:_isDown[1] and _isUp? 1:nz(_direction[1])
        _low2=ta.lowest(2)
        _high2 = ta.highest(2)
        _zigzag = _isUp[1] and _isDown and _direction[1] != -1?
        _high2: _isDown[1] and _isUp and _direction[1] != 1? _low2: na
```

```
sz = zigzag()
plot(sz,title='zigzag',color=color.blue,linewidth=2)
```

ANALYSIS LISTING IN.11

In the version 5 code shown, the version is denoted by comment lines preceding the actual code. If a version is not specified, Pine Script will automatically choose a version based on the code's needs. The significant variances between version 5 code and version 2 code are outlined below:

1.   In version 5, the study function name has been replaced with indicator.

2.   The lowest and highest functions have been renamed to ta.highest and ta.lowest in version 5.

3.   When trying to compile the version 2 script in version 5, an error arises, with the initial error cropping up on line 9 of the version 2 code: "Undeclared identifier '_direction'." This error indicates the utilization of a variable without prior declaration, a functionality allowed in version 2 but not in version 3 and beyond. To rectify this, _direction must be transformed into a mutable variable, initialized before utilization, and assigned a value using the := sign.

4.   Now, the code might execute; however, it issues a warning regarding the use of the ta.highest and ta.lowest functions with each execution. Additionally, the resulting plot does not meet the requirements. Therefore, you should extract the ta.lowest and ta.highest functions from the ternary conditional statement and execute them separately. This adjustment is made to enhance efficiency in PineScript.

5.   Look at the color argument in the plot function; version 2 can accept colors as 'blue', 'red', and 'green'; however, from version 4 onwards, system-defined color names have changed, and the color constant is written like color.blue, color.red etc, as values.

Identifying "BAT" Harmonic Pattern

Harmonic price patterns represent geometric formations on a chart, utilizing Fibonacci numbers to pinpoint precise turning points. These patterns are believed to be more prevalent in range-bound markets. Moreover, when they do occur in trending markets, harmonic patterns typically manifest against the prevailing trend.

Among the various harmonic patterns, the BAT pattern stands out. It comprises several distinct elements aiding its identification and contributes to defining a Potential Reversal Zone, as acknowledged by traders. This pattern assists in recognizing deep retests of support or resistance, often exhibiting sharp movements. Quick reversals from the Bat pattern's Potential Reversal Zone are quite common.

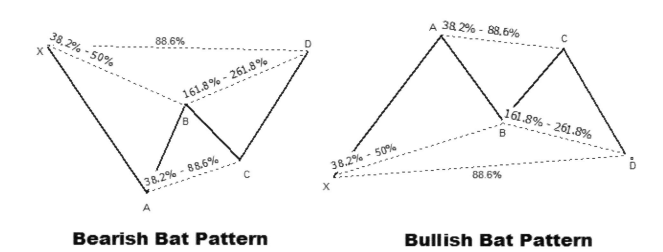

Bearish Bat Pattern   **Bullish Bat Pattern**

The Bat harmonic pattern consists of 5 swing points labeled X, A, B, C, and D. It can manifest as either a Bullish or Bearish bat, as illustrated in the figure above. In the case of the Bearish bat pattern, a short entry is initiated at point "D," whereas in the Bullish Bat Pattern, a long entry is taken at point D. This pattern typically necessitates a smaller stop loss during trading.

Regarding target levels, the initial target is set at 61.8% of the CD segment, followed by 1.272% of CD, and finally, the projection of XA from D, the entry point.

The Harmonic Bat pattern has the following characteristics that can be used to identify the pattern.
- AB leg retraces between 38.2% – 50% of XA leg
- BC leg retraces between 38.2% – 88.6% of AB leg
- CD leg retraces up to 88.6% of XA leg and CD leg also be an extension of between 1.618% – 2.618% of AB leg

I don't personally use harmonic patterns, and the definition above is borrowed from a trader. I've tried to code it here. Feel free to make any adjustments to ratios or other values as needed. Now, we'll proceed to write the code for identifying bat patterns on the chart based on the specified conditions.

INPUT & ANALYSIS LISTING IN.12 Identifying BAT

The initial segment of the code, up to line 18, is dedicated to creating and plotting zigzag indicators. We will now extend the preceding code. The latest identified zigzag occurrence is designated as the 'D' point of the BAT formation, while all past occurrences are labeled as x, a, b, and c. Lines 22 to 26 are utilized for storing the price values of x, a, b, c, and d points.

```
17: sz =  zigzag()
18: plot(sz, title='zigzag', color=color.blue, linewidth=2)
19:
20: //  ||---   Pattern Recognition:
21:
22: x = ta.valuewhen(sz, sz, 4)
23: a = ta.valuewhen(sz, sz, 3)
24: b = ta.valuewhen(sz, sz, 2)
25: c = ta.valuewhen(sz, sz, 1)
26: d = ta.valuewhen(sz, sz, 0)
27:
28: xab = (math.abs(b-a)/math.abs(x-a))
29: xad = (math.abs(a-d)/math.abs(x-a))
30: abc = (math.abs(b-c)/math.abs(a-b))
31: bcd = (math.abs(c-d)/math.abs(b-c))
```

The ta.valuewhen function is utilized in all these lines. The ta.valuewhen(condition, source, occurrence) function retrieves a value from the source series when the nth most recent occurrence of the condition was 'true'. It accepts three arguments: the condition, the source series from which information or value is sought, and the occurrence. The occurrence input is an integer. If the condition is 'true' for the nth occurrence in the past, the corresponding value from the source series is returned.

The below calculation is for a crossover; a boolean value is stored in the "cross_result" variable.

```
cross_result = ta.crossover(sma3,sma7)
```

In the example, the value of 'cross_over' would be 'true' only if a crossover has occurred; otherwise, its value would be false. The 'cross_result' is a series variable, and the calculation is performed for each bar as illustrated in the table:

Bar number	cross_result
0	True (zero recent occurrences)
1	False
2	False
3	True (first recent occurrence)
4	False

Suppose you now desire information about when the last crossover occurred, specifically the most recent occurrence of crossover. Let's assume you want the volume value of the last crossover. You can utilize:

```
last_vol = ta.valuewhen(cross_result,volume,1)
```

If you wish to obtain the volume at the time of the third most recent crossover that might have occurred, you can adjust the occurrence number to 3. It's important to note that any value greater than or equal to 1 is considered 'true', while zero, negative values, and 'na' are considered false.

Now, examine the code lines from 22 to 26. In this segment, the variable "d" retains the most recent price value obtained from the zigzag indicator and is designated as "d". Likewise, the second-to-last pivot's price value is stored in the variable 'c', and so on. This approach guarantees that we have the price values of x, a, b, c, and d.

```
32:
33: // ||--> Functions:
34: isBat()=>
35:    _xab = xab >= 0.382 and xab <= 0.5
36:    _abc = abc >= 0.382 and abc <= 0.886
37:    _bcd = bcd >= 1.618 and bcd <= 2.618
38:    _xad = xad <= 0.618 and xad <= 1.000
39:    _result_var = _xab and _abc and _bcd and _xad
40:    _result_var
41:
42: plotshape(isBat(), text="Bat", title=", style=shape.labeldown, color=color.maroon,
```

> textcolor=color.white, location=location.top, offset=0)

The corresponding ratios are computed from lines 28 to 31. A new function, 'math.abs', is introduced here. The "math.abs" function, commonly known as the absolute function, converts negative values into positive values while leaving positive numbers unchanged. The length of the AB arm of the pattern is determined by subtracting the values of 'a' and 'b'. The abs function ensures that the result is always a positive number. You can review how the ratios are calculated.

Line 34 introduces the BAT function; it calculates the BAT function using all the conditions defined in the specifications. The Fibonacci ratio numbers specified in the definitions are applied here. The _result_var is set to 'true' only if all the aforementioned conditions are satisfied.

Line 42 contains a plotshape function; it displays the text "BAT" when the condition is 'true'.
OUTPUT LISTING IN.12

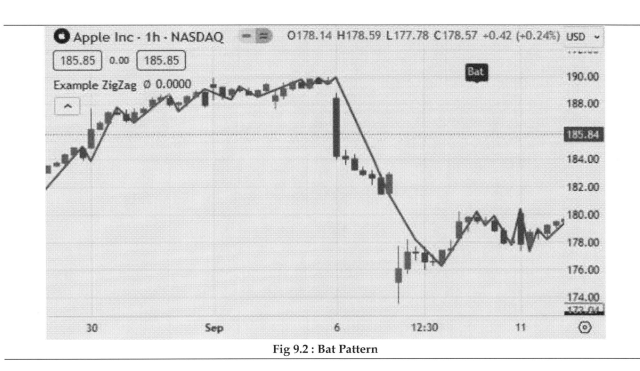

Fig 9.2 : Bat Pattern

These are not so easy to discover; however, I have found one on an hourly chart. Whether this is bullish or bearish BAT? You can always find it out by checking the value of D compared to C, if D is more than C, it is bearish, and if D is less than C, it is a bullish BAT pattern.

Summary

- The Zig Zag indicator connects the highest and lowest points on the chart by a straight line whenever prices reverse.
- The 'nz' function is used as filler to replace all 'na' values with zeros
- The ta.valuewhen(condition, source, occurrence) function provides value from source series when the nth most recent occurrence of condition was true
- BAT is a geometric price pattern on a chart that uses Fibonacci numbers to define precise turning points.
- The math.abs function can take integers and float as arguments. The math.abs function ensures that a result is a positive number. It converts all negative values to positive ones, and no changes are made to positive values.

Quiz

Q1. Study the below code:

```
a= 1
b= 2
b= a+b
```

What is the error, and how can it be solved?

Q2. Consider the following code:

```
myFun(a, b, c)=>
Z = a+b –c
Z

X = 2
Y = 3
Z = 9
T = myFun(X,Y,Z)
```

What would be the value of T?

Q3. Suppose a variable series "myVar" is represented visually as under:

5	7	na	9	6	na	0	3	2	1

How can you replace all 'na' with zeros?

Chapter -10: Built-in line function

Technical analysis lines are primarily utilized to illustrate support, resistance, or trend on charts, which traders often find necessary. PineScript provides a built-in function for drawing lines. In this section, we will delve into the fundamentals of line functions and examine various examples. Throughout the examples, we will also explore several built-in functions and variables. Consequently, the chapter is divided into the following sections.

- Line Function
- Example joining pivot points
  - The pivothigh function
  - The pivotlow function

Line Function

A line is formed by connecting two distinct points. This connection between points delineates a line segment, with one point serving as the starting point and the other as the endpoint. Every line on a chart, regardless of its slope or orientation, adheres to this fundamental principle.

In charting, each point is defined by two essential values: price and time. Price indicates the specific value of an asset at a given point in time, while time denotes the moment when the price is observed. Together, these two values pinpoint the precise location of a point on the chart.

Therefore, the creation and interpretation of lines on a chart are rooted in the relationship between points, which are characterized by their price and time coordinates.

If I ask you to locate a point on a chart or a graph paper, I must tell you the price and the time. Once you know these two, you can go to the specific time, locate the price, and mark your point. Similarly, for drawing a line, you must know two values of the starting point and two for the endpoints. Based on this concept, the syntax or format to use a line function is as under:

```
line.new(x1, y1, x2, y2, xloc, extend, color, style, width)
```

In the syntax provided, the variables x1 and y1 represent the coordinates of the starting point, while x2 and y2 denote the coordinates of the endpoint for the line you intend to draw. In this context, y1 and y2 correspond to the price values, which are plotted along the y-axis of the chart. On the other hand, x1 and x2 may represent either time values or bar numbers, which defines the horizontal position of the points along the x-axis. The horizontal position can either be represented in time or numerical identifiers for bars on the chart. By specifying these coordinates, position lines can be drawn on the chart for technical analysis.

The bar_index is a built-in variable that stores the number assigned to each bar on a chart. The bar indexing starts from 0, representing the first historical bar. Consequently, the bar_index for the initial historical bar is always set to zero. The most recent bar's index corresponds to bar_index.

Another argument utilized in the line function is xloc, which can accept either xloc.bar_index or xloc.bar_time as input. By default, it is set to xloc.bar_index. If you're specifying x1 and x2 values based on bar_index, you should use xloc.bar_index; however, if you're utilizing UNIX timestamp as time input, you should opt for xloc.bar_time. Personally, I prefer using xloc.bar_index.

For instance, if I intend to draw a short horizontal line on each bar where 'y' equals 2% of the 'open' price, and I choose to use xloc.bar_index, the line would commence from the midpoint of the current bar and conclude at the midpoint of the next adjacent bar. The figure illustrates the outcome of such scripting. It's impractical to position line drawings or any other drawings between the two bars.

Utilizing bar_index allows us to place our line directly on the bar with the specified number. However, in numerous cases, time values are more readily available and convenient for plotting purposes.

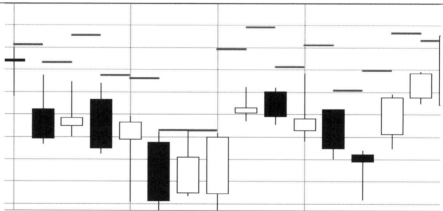

Fig 10.1: Line not exactly above the bar

The subsequent argument in the line function is 'extend', which can accept values from extend.none, extend.right, extend.left, and extend.both. However, the default value is extend.none.

When extend.none is selected, a line is drawn starting from point (x1, y1) and ending at point (x2, y2). If extend is set to extend.right or extend.left, the line becomes a ray that originates from either point (x1, y1) or (x2, y2), respectively. Setting extend=extend.both results in drawing an infinite line passing through both points.

We have already covered color and width, so they are not being discussed here.

The final argument under consideration is 'style'. The available options for style include line.style_solid, line.style_dotted, line.style_dashed, line.style_arrow_left, line.style_arrow_right, and line.style_arrow_both. As implied by the name, the style attribute alters the appearance of lines. I encourage you to experiment with these different styles.

Below is the example code utilizing xloc.bar_index for the figure presented earlier in this chapter:

```
//@version=5
indicator("Example Xloc.bar_index", overlay=true)
line.new(bar_index-1,open*1.02,bar_index,open*1.02,xloc=xloc.bar_index,width=2)
```

The code is straight forward and therefore no explanation is being provided.

Now, we attempt to draw the line on the bar using the xloc.bar_time argument value for xloc. Before we delve into using xloc.bar_time, I'd like to introduce two additional built-in variables: "time" and "time_close". As their names suggest, "time" provides the current time, while "time_close" furnishes the time of the bar's close in UNIX format. This UNIX format represents the number of milliseconds elapsed since 00:00:00 UTC on 1 January 1970. It's a substantial number, and for practical purposes, we'll rely on the built-in variables time and time_close to represent time without the need for manual calculation.

INPUT LISTING IN.13 Line drawing using xloc.bar_time argument

```
01: //@version=5
02: indicator("Example Xloc.bar_time", overlay=true)
03: //calculate one day (in milliseconds)
04: day1 = 1000 * 24*60*60
05: line.new(time,open*1.02,time-day1,open*1.02,xloc=xloc.bar_time,width=2)
```

OUTPUT LISTING IN.13 Line drawing using xloc.bar_time argument

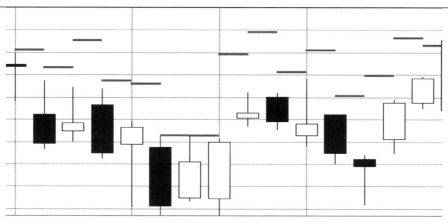

Fig 10.2 : Plot using xloc.bar_time

ANALYSIS LISTING IN.13 Line drawing using xloc.bar_time argument

Here is the explanation of code:

The **'day1 = 1000 * 24*60*60'** calculates the length of one day in milliseconds. There are 1000 milliseconds in one second, 60 seconds in one minute, 60 minutes in one hour, and 24 hours in one day.

The code **"line.new(time,open*1.02,time-day1,open*1.02,xloc=xloc.bar_time,width=2)"** creates a new horizontal line on the chart. Let's break down the parameters:

- time: The starting time for the line. In this case, it's the current bar's time.
- open*1.02: The starting price for the line. It's calculated by multiplying the opening price (open) by 1.02, which increases it by 2%.
- time-day1: The ending time for the line, which is the current time minus one day (specified by day1).
- open*1.02: The ending price for the line, which is the same as the starting price.
- xloc=xloc.bar_time: This parameter sets the horizontal alignment of the line based on the bar's time. It ensures that the line extends from the current bar's time to one day prior.
- width=2: This parameter sets the width of the line to 2 pixels.
- The xloc.bar_time parameter specifies that the horizontal alignment of the line should be based on the time of the bars. It ensures that the line is drawn from the current bar's time to one day prior, allowing you to visualize a range over the past day.

Example joining pivot points

Pivot points represent significant swing high and swing low points on a price chart graph. Similar to zigzag indicators, they help identify crucial turning points in the market. Pivot points are considered lagging indicators, which means pivot high or low points are recognized only after the price has experienced a notable shift in direction. This lagging nature of pivot points underscores their reliance on historical price data and their tendency to confirm trends or reversals rather than predict them in real-time. Traders often use pivot points to gauge potential support and resistance levels and to make informed decisions based on past price movements.

The pine script has separate inbuilt functions for pivot high(ta.pivothigh) and pivot low(ta.pivotlow) to return the price of pivot high or low points. It returns 'NaN' if there was no pivot point.

The ta.pivothigh function
As discussed earlier, the ta.pivothigh function returns a high swing price or 'nan' if there is no high pivot point. The ta.pivothigh function has three arguments.

```
ta.pivothigh(source, leftbars, rightbars)
```

A high is labelled as a swing high by the pivot functions after a certain number of bars defined by leftbars and rightbars variables have happened before and after a possible recent high.

The ta.pivotlow function

Similar to ta.pivothigh function, the ta.pivotlow function returns a low swing price or 'nan' if there is no low pivot point. The ta.pivotlow function also has three arguments.

```
ta.pivotlow(source, leftbars, rightbars)
```

The source in both ta.pivotlow and ta.pivothigh is optional. By default, for ta.pivothigh, "high" variable is the default, and for ta.pivotlow,"low" is the default variable for source. Practically, there is no use of a source, and we can leave it.

Now that we have a function for calculating swing high and low, we can mark the points on the chart.

INPUT LISTING IN.14 Marking Pivot Points

```
01: // This source code is subject to the terms of the Mozilla Public License 2.0
02: // © Teach Yourself Trade Strategies in PineScript
03: //@version=5
04: indicator("Example-Pivot marking", overlay=true)
05:
06: ///code for Pivot Point///
```

```
07: leftBars  = 4 //left strength
08: rightBars = 2 //right strenght

09:
10: swh = ta.pivothigh(leftBars, rightBars)
11: swl = ta.pivotlow(leftBars, rightBars)
12:
13: swh_cond = not na(swh)
14: swl_cond = not na(swl)
15:
16: plotshape(swh_cond, text = "PH", color = color.green,
17:   style = shape.arrowdown, location = location.abovebar, offset = -rightBars)
18: plotshape(swl_cond, text = "PL", color = color.red,
19:   style = shape.arrowup,   location = location.belowbar, offset = -rightBars)
```

OUTPUT LISTING IN.14 Marking Pivot Points

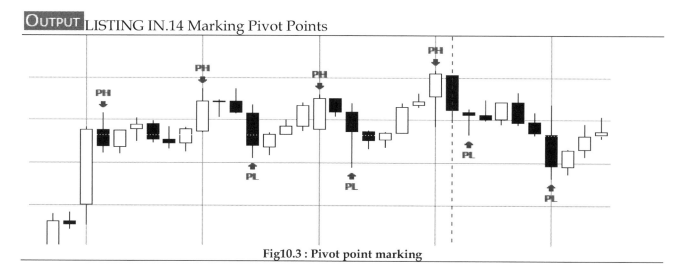

Fig10.3 : Pivot point marking

ANALYSIS LISTING IN.14 Marking Pivot Points

Line 7 and 8 declare and initialize variables used in the pivot functions. In line 10, "swh" is a float series and stores the value of pivot high only if it finds pivot as per the leftbar and right bar strengths. If there is no pivot high, the value of "swh" remains 'NaN,' i.e. nothing.

In simpler terms, "swh" is a series that looks like

Bar no	234	235	236	237	238	239	240
Swh	NaN	NaN	NaN	NaN	234.5	NaN	NaN

The "swh" have a value when there is a pivot high, i.e. a pivot high at bar no 238, and the high pivot price is 234.5; all other values are 'NaN'. However, this series would be considered a float series.

Similarly, line 11 stores the pivot value low in variable "swl".

Line 13 defines a new variable boolean swh_cond. The swh_cond is 'true' if "swh" does not have a 'NaN' value. The right-hand side of the statement is 'not na(swh)'. You already know that not is a logical operator.

Similarly, in line 14, the value of swl_cond is 'true' only if "swl" has a value suggesting a low pivot point.

Line 16 & 17 contains a single statement, and line 18 & 19 contains another single statement. The statements are in two lines providing indentation of two spaces instead of the standard tab or 4 spaces for the second line.

In lines 16 to 19, the plotshape function is utilized as discussed in earlier lessons. In this case, the offset parameter has been set to zero. The pivot markings appear two bars ahead of the actual pivot highs and lows because the pivot functions have been invoked with the argument rightBars=2. The system identifies a pivot high or low only after analyzing data from two bars. To rectify this issue, we should adjust the offset to -rightBars. This adjustment ensures that the pivot markings align accurately with the actual pivot highs and lows without the two-bar delay.

INPUT LISTING IN.15 Joining pivot points

```
20: ///------------Marking Ends------------------
21:
22: high1 = ta.valuewhen(swh_cond,swh,1)
23: high2 = ta.valuewhen(swh_cond,swh,0)
24: bar_h1 = ta.valuewhen(swh_cond, bar_index-rightBars,1)
25: bar_h2 = ta.valuewhen(swh_cond,bar_index-rightBars,0)
26:
27: line.new(x1=bar_h1, y1=high1, x2=bar_h2, y2=high2,xloc=xloc.bar_index,
```

```
28:    extend=extend.none,color=color.blue)
29:
30: low1 = ta.valuewhen(swl_cond,swl,1)
31: low2 = ta.valuewhen(swl_cond,swl,0)
32: bar_l1 = ta.valuewhen(swl_cond, bar_index-rightBars,1)
33: bar_l2 = ta.valuewhen(swl_cond,bar_index-rightBars,0)
34:
35: line.new(x1=bar_l1, y1=low1, x2=bar_l2, y2=low2,xloc=xloc.bar_index,
36:    extend=extend.none,color=color.red)
```

Till line no 19, code of LISTING IN.14 is used.

OUTPUT LISTING IN.15 Joining Pivot Points

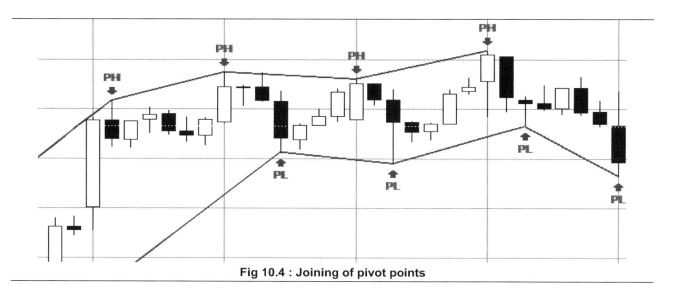

Fig 10.4 : Joining of pivot points

ANALYSIS LISTING IN.15 Joining pivot points

Till line no 19, code of LISTING IN.14 is used. In the 'plotshape' function offset value has been set to -rightBars as discussed in the previous section.

Line 22 to 25, we have used the 'ta.valuewhen' function to obtain the value of pivot high and bar index for the recent pivot high and the one before the recent occurrence. As we have already discussed in previous lessons, ta.valuewhen provides the value of from the source list when the condition is 'true' for the nth occurrence. The format or syntax for the formula is as under:

```
result_value = ta.valuewhen(source, condition, occurrence)
```

On line no 22, 'high1 = ta.valuewhen(swh_cond,swh,1)', high1 variable would store value of swh for last occurrence, when swh_cond is true. Similarly, the value of high2 is calculated.

On line 24, bar_h1 would store value of bar_index - rightBars. Rightbars have been deducted from the bar_index value because when "swh" becomes true, the chart has moved two bars in opposite directions.

Since we already have the coordinates for both points, we are able to draw the line. The inputs **x1, y1, x2**, and **y2** represent the coordinates of the two points for the line. In this context, we have computed the points for the recent swing high, denoted as **high2** and **bar_h2**, while the points for the swing high just prior to this instance are represented by **high1** and **bar_h1**. We provide the values of these points to the line function in order to draw the line segment. This allows us to visually connect the swing highs on the chart, providing insight into the price movement pattern. The **xloc** value can take only one of the two values i.e. **xloc.bar_index** or **xloc.bar_time**. In this script, we are since using **bar_index** as input for x -the axis; we would use **xloc.bar_index**.

We have set **extend=extend.none**, though the argument is optional and the default value is also extend.none, we have provided the same to the function for illustration purposes. Another argument is "**color**", which is optional.

We have used the same methodology for plotting pivot low on lines 30 to 36. You can use variable names of your choice.

Summary

- Every line has one starting point and one endpoint.
- The bar_index is an inbuilt variable that stores the number of the bar. The bar indexing starts from 0 for the first historical bar. The latest bar index is bar_index
- The time_close function provides the time of the bar's close in UNIX format. The UNIX time format is the number of milliseconds that have elapsed since 00:00:00 UTC, 1 January 1970.
- If the line is plotted using x-axis values as the time, we have to set the xloc argument to xloc.bar_time. If you use the x-axis value as bar_index, the xloc argument should be set to xloc.bar_index.
- The ta.pivothigh and ta.pivotlow functions are inbuilt functions of pine script to calculate swing high and swing low values.

Quiz

Q1. What if the xloc value is not defined in the line function? What is the default value for the xloc function?

Q2. What is the default value of the "extend" argument in the line function?

Q3.What are the compulsory arguments of line function?

Exercise

Q. Is the zigzag function calculation in the previous lesson and pivot high and pivot low with rightBar =1 and leftBar= 1 giving the same result?

(Hint draw zigzag function on the chart and also mark pivot high and pivot low on the same chart)

Chapter -11: Customizable script - Taking input from users

Users frequently tailor indicators to meet their specific needs. For instance, if you add a Simple Moving Average (SMA) to your chart with a default period of 9, you always have the freedom to adjust the period to 7 or any other value that better suits your requirements by accessing the indicator's settings. You anticipate having the flexibility within the settings to modify all or some of the parameters.

As a user, you should have the ability to alter the length of the moving average, the data source for the moving average, or the color of the moving average line within the indicator's settings or options. These adjustments constitute user-defined inputs, and there typically exists a default value if a user does not provide input.

Up to this point, none of the codes we've discussed have included an option for modifying or defining parameters. Now, let's execute our code LISTING IN.5, which identifies Doji patterns on a candlestick chart, and examine the settings. What options do we encounter? We're presented with the option to adjust the color of shapes or objects drawn on the chart under the 'style' section. However, what if we desire to grant users the flexibility to modify the tolerance value between the open and close prices?

The input function

In Pine Script, the input function enables users to adjust parameters permitted by the script's author. To redefine the variable tolerance to allow user-defined values, insert the following line into the Doji script in place of the tolerance value:

```
tolerance = input(defval = 0.05)/100
```

With this line, users can now modify the tolerance parameter according to their preferences. The tolerance variable is where the value is stored. It is positioned on the left-hand side of the assignment operator. After the equal sign (=), which denotes the assignment operator, we employ the input function on the right-hand side. This input function accepts a float value.

We intend to maintain the default value at 0.05%, offering users the option to adjust it. The 'defvalue' argument within the input function establishes 0.05 as the default value. By integrating this code into the chart and navigating to its settings, users can modify the value of the Tolerance parameter.

To enhance clarity and provide users with a better understanding of the variable's purpose, it's essential to choose descriptive variable names. Additionally, specifying whether the input represents a percentage or a multiplier can prevent confusion among users.

To address these concerns, you can utilize the 'title' argument within the input function to describe the parameter in place of the variable's name. Here's how you can adjust the code for the DOJI open-to-close tolerance.

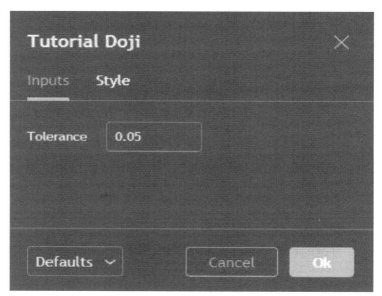

Fig11.1: Input window under settings of Indicator

tolerance = input(defval=0.05, title="Doji open to close tolerance")/100

In the updated line of code, 'tolerance' serves as the variable name. The 'title' argument provides a descriptive label for the parameter, indicating that it is **"Doji open to close tolerance"**. Users can easily understand and adjust this parameter within the chart settings.

Now, a pertinent question arises: What if a user inadvertently messes up my code? What if they input zero or ten thousand? What if users aren't aware of the appropriate range for a given parameter? Data validation becomes crucial before integrating them into the script.

You might have encountered scenarios on websites where you're required to fill out forms. As you enter numbers and names, the system may throw errors upon submission, such as a phone number must be 10 characters long, or names cannot contain numbers. These scripts serve to filter client-side data, preventing unrealistic values or data from entering the system and causing errors. In Pine Script, we can also implement filters to ensure that user-entered data is accurate, within the designated range, and realistic.

For adding range limits to the data, we can add two additional augments to the input function, i.e. 'minval' and 'maxval'. As the name suggests, they provide lower and upper range limits. The 'minval' is defined as .01 and 'maxval' as 1.

Now my new code in version 4 or below is as under:

```
tolerance = input(defval=0.05,title="Doji open to close
    tolerance",minval=.01,maxval=1)/100
```

In version 5, it's necessary to specify the input type as either integer or float before utilizing maxval or minval as arguments. We'll delve into this topic further in the upcoming sections. Additionally, I'll cover codes for version 4 because understanding them might be necessary if you need to modify code written in version 4.

After implementing the aforementioned adjustments and adding them to the chart, you won't notice any visual changes. However, users are now restricted from inputting values greater than 1 or less than 0.01. This restriction ensures that users don't input unrealistic numbers. Nevertheless, users may still be unaware of the minimum increment allowed for user input.

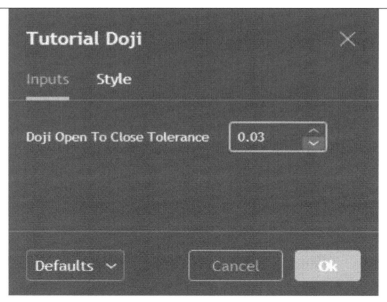

Fig11.2: Input window with custom title

Using the 'step' argument, we can specify the minimum incremental value within an input function. The code for version 4 is as follows:

tolerance = input(defval=0.05,title="Doji open to close tolerance", minval=.01, maxval=1, step=.01) /100

After integrating this code into the chart, users have two sliders to facilitate value adjustments with step increments. While the sliders were present in previous iterations of the code, they weren't operational. Now, they function correctly, enabling users to adjust values incrementally by 0.01.

The official Pine Script manual provides several helpful examples for utilizing these input functions. Additionally, you can employ the "type" argument within input functions for certain data validation purposes.

Boolean input provides a toggle button

In version 5 of Pine Script, if you wish to receive Boolean input, you can utilize the input.bool() function. In older versions, you may specify the type as "bool" in the input function, like so: type=input.bool. Toggle buttons are presented to users under the input window for their selection.

It's worth noting that using input.bool does not support the "minval", "maxval", and "step" arguments, as it's primarily designed for Boolean inputs.

Version 4
first_example = input(title="On/Off", type=input.bool, defval=true)

Version 5
first_example = input.bool(title="On/Off", defval=true)

Integer input

The code for integer input is similar to the one we discussed in the doji example; however, if the type is set to an integer, then a user would not be able to input decimal values. The example code is as under:

Version 4
integer_input = input(title="integer_input", type=input.integer, defval=7, minval=-10, maxval=10)

Version 5
integer_input = input.integer(title="integer_input", defval=7, minval=-10, maxval=10)

Float input

The code for float input is similar to the one we discussed in the doji example; however, if the type is set to float, then the user would not be able to input alphabets. The example code is as under:

Version 4
f = input(title="take profit per cent", type=input.float, defval=0.5, minval=0, maxval=5.5, step=0.02)

Version 5
f = input.float(title="take profit per cent", defval=0.5, minval=0, maxval=5.5, step=0.02)

Symbol input

The symbol input type allows users to input any script symbol recognized or supported by TradingView. Below is an example where the input type is a symbol, and the default value is set to "DELL"..

Version 4
sym = input(title="Symbol", type=input.symbol, defval="DELL")

Version 5
sym = input.symbol(title="Symbol", defval="DELL")

Resolution input

The resolution represents the timeframe you intend to use. The input.resolution type offers a drop-down menu of all available time frames for selection. Below is an example of type "resolution" with the input "defval" set to 60::

Version 4
res = input(title="Resolution", type=input.resolution, defval="60")

Version 5
res = input(title="Resolution", defval="60")

Source input

The input.source type presents a drop-down menu that allows users to select a source from various built-in options like open, high, low, close, volume, hl2, hlc3, ohlc4, etc. Below is an example code for both versions 4 and 5:

Version 4
src = input(title="Source", type=input.source, defval=close)

Version 5
src = input.source(title="Source", defval=close)

Option argument of the input function

The The 'option' is another argument available for the input function. Rather than allowing users to input their preferred value manually, it offers a dropdown menu where users can select values from a list provided by the author. For instance, in the example below for sessions, the default value is set to 24X7, and the author has provided options. Users can select from these options in a dropdown menu:

Version 4
SessionDetails = input(title="Session", defval="0900-1300", options=["24x7", "0900-1300", "1300-1700", "1700-2100"])

Version 5
SessionDetails = input(title="Session", defval="0900-1300", options=["24x7", "0900-1300", "1300-1700", "1700-2100"])

If you use an "option" argument in the input function, I suggest not using 'minval', 'maxval' or 'step' arguments.

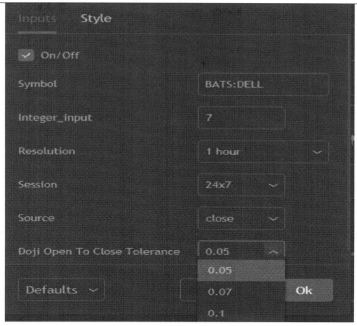

Fig: Input window with an option argument

Now the above code is modified and I have provided three options to users for selecting a value. Users would not be allowed to input any arbitrary number other than the number defined in the script.

Version 4
tolerance = input(defval=0.05,title="Doji open to close tolerance",options=[0.05,0.07,0.1])
Version 5
tolerance = input.float(defval=0.05,title="Doji open to close tolerance",options=[0.05,0.07,0.1])

Now users would have the option to select; a user cannot key in values.

I hope the numerous parameters of the "input" function haven't confused you. The input function offers various features like types, options, minval, maxval, and step arguments to prevent users from entering unrealistic values that could cause errors in the script, whether due to ignorance or otherwise. The only essential argument you need to provide is the 'defval'.

You don't need to memorize all the options available in the input function for validating user input. However, it's beneficial to understand the capabilities of the PineScript language. At any time, you can simply press Ctrl and click on the name of a built-in function or variable to access detailed information from the reference manual.

Summary

- Taking input from users makes code more flexible for use by users.
- The input function has built-in types for validating data and ensuring input values are within the desired range.
- The input function provides options in the indicator's setting section to change a value for the variables allowed by the coder to change.
- At any point in time, you can always press Ctrl and click on the name of a built-in function or variable to get details from the reference manual.

Quiz

Q1. Study the below code of line

```
src = input(defval= 5,title="Take Profit")
```

would the above code allows a user to input a value of 6.6?

Q2. Change the above code to have integers from 2 to 8.

Q3. For the code

```
f = input(title="Level", type=XXXX, defval=5, minval=0,
    maxval=10, step=0.02)
```

What is the value of type?

Exercise

Q1. Write a program to plot two SMAs for cross-over. Provide options to users to change the length and source of each SMA.

Chapter -12: Indicators & code library

This lesson serves as a tour of the indicators accessible in Pine Script and an introduction to the community library of codes and indicators. If you've already reviewed these materials, feel free to take a glance and skip ahead.

Built-in Indicators

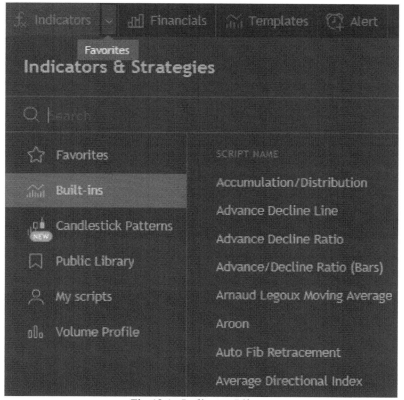

Fig 12.1 : Indicator Library

Pinescript has various built-in indicators. The list of Built-in scripts is available in Built-in under the Indicator tab. You can select any built-in indicator or indicator provided by other pinescript authors for your use.

I choose Aroon for myself by clicking on it.

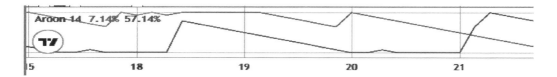

Now click on source code, and the source code for the built-in function 'aroon' appears in the pine editor. However, until you save and make it yours, you won't be able to edit the source code.

```
1  //@version=5
2  indicator(title="Aroon", shorttitle="Aroon", overlay=false, format=format.percent
3  length = input.int(14, minval=1)
4  upper = 100 * (ta.highestbars(high, length+1) + length)/length
5  lower = 100 * (ta.lowestbars(low, length+1) + length)/length
6  plot(upper, "Aroon Up", color=#FB8C00)
7  plot(lower, "Aroon Down", color=#2962FF)
```

The source code for some built-in functions may not be accessible, but for most indicators, the source code is available, enabling users to grasp the underlying logic of the indicators.

Similarly, every Pine Script user has the option to publish and share their code with the public. TradingView coders can also publish their results and permit others to use the script while keeping the indicator's source code hidden.

In the 'Public Library' under the 'Indicators and Strategy' dropdown menu, all the scripts published by users are displayed. Users can select any script for their own use. Personally, I tend to prefer scripts with more likes. After the script name, you'll see the author's name and the number of likes, as demonstrated below.

Madrid Moving Average Ribbon	Madrid	21800
Candlestick Patterns Identified (updated 3/11/15)	repo32	20368
Swing high low support & resistance, by Patterns...	Patternsmart	20191

When hovering over an indicator name and seeing '{ }', it indicates that the code is publicly viewable. Conversely, if '{ }' does not appear, the code is not public. To apply the indicator to the chart, simply click on the indicator.

After adding the code to the chart, you can click on '{ }' next to the indicator's name on the chart to view its source code. To edit the source code, you need to save it by clicking the save button on the Pine Editor.

As discussed in earlier sections, scripts may exist in earlier versions. Therefore, exercise caution when using parts of code or functions from earlier versions of Pine Script in your current version.

Publishing Code to Trading View

On the right corner of the Pine Editor, there's a "Publish" button that enables you to share your code with the community. It's advisable to publish your script only when you're confident about its content and intend to do so. Once published, TradingView does not offer an option to remove or hide the script. Therefore, it's important to consider carefully before making your script public.

Request from Readers

If you found my book helpful and it contributed positively to your learning experience, I kindly request you to consider leaving feedback and a rating for the book on the Amazon website. As an author, receiving feedback and ratings not only keeps me motivated but also helps to increase book sales. Your support is greatly appreciated. Thank you for considering providing your feedback.

Chapter 13: Errors and their remedy

While coding your scripts, you may encounter various difficulties in the form of compilation errors. Each error is unique and offers new insights during the correction process. To help you overcome compiling difficulties, I'm providing some frequently occurring errors in Pine Script.

The console window below your code displays the error messages. Version 5 of Pine Script provides more detailed error information compared to previous versions, making error discovery easier. I strongly recommend using version 5 for better error detection and resolution..

Cannot be used as a variable or function name: The error "Cannot be used as a variable or function name" occurs when a user attempts to use a reserved keyword as the name of a variable or function. Since TradingView's system already employs the term '**range**', users must choose a different name for their variable to resolve this issue.

```
1  //@version=5
2  indicator("Tutorial Doji",overlay = true)
3  tolerance = 0.02/100
4  range = high-low
5  Is_OC_Equal = (open > close  and open < close*(1 + tolerance)) or
6    (open < close and open > close*(1-tolerance)) ?true:false
7  range:=Is_OC_Equal
8  plotshape(Is_OC_Equal)
```

```
Script study added to the chart
Add to Chart operation failed, reason: line 4: 'range' cannot be
used as a variable or function name
```

Cannot assign expression of type: The error arises when a variable attempts to store a value of a different data type. For instance, trying to assign a string to an integer variable or a boolean result to an integer variable would trigger this error. It's important to ensure that variables are assigned values consistent with their data type to avoid this issue.

Here is a code to explain the issue:

```
1  //@version=5
2  indicator("Tutorial Doji",overlay = true)
3  tolerance = 0.02/100
4  range1 = high-low
5  Is_OC_Equal = (open > close  and open < close*(1 + tolerance)) or
6    (open < close and open > close*(1-tolerance)) ?true:false
7  range1:=Is_OC_Equal
8  plotshape(Is_OC_Equal)
```

```
Add to Chart operation failed, reason: line 7: Variable 'range1' was
declared with 'series float' type. Cannot assign it expression of
type 'series bool'.
```

In the provided code, line no. 7 attempts to assign the boolean variable Is_OC_Equal to the float variable range1. However, a datatype mismatch error occurs because Is_OC_Equal is of type boolean (series bool), while range1 is of type float (series float).

The system has generated the error "cannot assign it an expression of type 'series bool'". Additionally, it has indicated that the variable range1 is of type 'series float'. To resolve this datatype mismatch error, ensure that variables being assigned are of compatible types. In this case, you may need to modify either Is_OC_Equal or range1 to ensure they have matching data types.

Cannot call with arguments: The error "Cannot call with arguments" occurs when there are issues with the arguments provided to a function. This error can stem from several causes:

- Incorrect order of arguments.
- Insufficient number of arguments provided.
- Incorrect or incompatible argument provided.

To resolve this error, ensure that the arguments passed to the function are in the correct order, all required arguments are provided, and each argument is of the appropriate type and format expected by the function. Double-checking the function documentation or examples may also help identify any discrepancies in argument usage.

COULD NOT FIND FUNCTION:

```
1   //@version=5
2   indicator("Tutorial Doji",overlay = true)
3   myEMA = ta.ema1(close,7)
4   plot(myEMA)
```

```
Add to Chart operation failed, reason: line 3: Could
not find function or function reference 'ta.ema1'.
```

The error "Could not find function or function reference 'ema1'" occurs when a function is either not defined in the script or there is a typo in the function name.

In the example provided, the code attempts to call a function named 'ema1' instead of 'ema'. As a result, the compiler cannot find the 'ema1' function, leading to the error message.

The hint provided by the compiler is helpful in identifying the location of the error, which in this case is at line number 3 where the 'ema1' function is referenced. To resolve this issue, correct the function name to 'ema' to match the actual function definition or ensure that the intended function is properly defined in the script.

END OF LINE WITHOUT CONTINUATION: The error occurs in PineScript when there is an issue with indentation. PineScript follows a convention where indentation consists of either 4 spaces or 1 tab for functions, loops, etc. If a statement is very long and needs to be split into two lines, non-standard indentation can be used. Typically, 2 spaces before the statement line are preferred.

In cases of indentation problems, the system may interpret the last line as continuing, leading to this error. It's essential to ensure consistent and correct indentation throughout the script to avoid such errors.

Below is an example of such an error.

```
1   //@version=5
2   indicator("Tutorial Doji",overlay = true)
3   myEMA =
4   ta.ema(close,7)
5   plot(myEMA)
```

```
Add to Chart operation failed, reason: line 3:
Syntax error at input 'end of line without line continuation'.
```

In line 4, the statement was split into two lines, but proper indentation was not provided. Reviewing the code's indentation, especially near the line number provided by the console window, can help resolve this error. Ensuring consistent and correct indentation throughout the code is important to prevent such errors.

Loop is too long: The error "Loop is too long" can occur in Pine Script due to several reasons. Since Pine Script runs scripts from its server rather than the user's computer, resources are shared among various users.

This error may arise if the loop you're using is too lengthy and takes more time for execution than usual. Even if your loop is relatively small but requires intensive calculations, it might still trigger the error. Sometimes, coding errors can also contribute to this issue.

In such cases, it's advisable to review your code and algorithm, attempting to minimize the resources it consumes. Simplifying complex calculations and optimizing algorithms can help mitigate this error and improve script performance.

Mismatched input: The error "Mismatched input" occurs when there is a deviation from the correct syntax of the code. In the provided example, using '(' instead of ']' intentionally leads to this error.

The error message typically includes a line number and provides hints about the mistake made in the code. It's essential to carefully review the code and correct any syntax errors to resolve this issue..

```
1  //@version=5
2  indicator("Tutorial Doji",overlay = true)
3  myEMA = ta.ema(close,7]
4  plot(myEMA)

▼
Add to Chart operation failed, reason: line 3: Mismatched
input ']' expecting ')'.
```

These are since syntax errors, they require study of code vis-à-vis syntax and taking help of error line number and other details for solving them.

Out of depth at index: The error "Out of depth at index" occurs when a script attempts to generate a signal before having processed the required minimum number of bars. This often happens due to the complexity of the code or other factors.

To resolve this issue, add the max_bars_back argument to your script's indicator() or strategy() function. Set the value of max_bars_back equal to the minimum number of bars your script requires for signal generation. This ensures that the script has processed a sufficient number of bars before attempting to generate signals.

Pine cannot determine the referencing length of a series: In some cases, this error is generated. It can be solved by including `max_bars_back = 100 or 300` in indicator()/strategy() declaration statement. The system fails to ascertain the number of minimum bars required for calculation. For example, if you are calculating ta.ema(close,7), then you would need 7 bars at least to generate a result. But sometimes, your script may use such codes that the system fails to understand the number of bars required.

The script must have at least one output function call: The error "The script must have at least one output function call" occurs when a script, whether it's an indicator script or a strategy script, does not generate any output or result. This means that the script neither plots on a chart nor provides orders to the system.

To resolve this error, it's necessary to generate some form of output, such as plots, drawings, or backtest results, within the script. This ensures that the script produces meaningful output and can be successfully compiled.

The script must have one indicator() or strategy() function call: check the first line of code, the error generates when you have not put an indicator() or strategy() function as the first line of code.

Undeclared identifier: The error "Undeclared identifier" occurs when a variable is used without being declared or defined in the script. This error message typically provides the variable's name and the line number where the error occurred in the console window.

This error can occur due to a typo in the variable name, causing the system to interpret it as a new variable instead of the intended one. To resolve this issue, ensure that all variables are properly declared and spelled correctly throughout the script. Reviewing the code for any typos or missing variable declarations can help mitigate this error.

```
1  //@version=5
2  indicator("Tutorial Doji",overlay = true)
3  lenght = 7
4  myEMA = ta.ema(close,length)
5  plot(myEMA)

Add to Chart operation failed, reason: line 4: Undeclared
identifier 'length'
```

In the provided script, a variable named "length" is defined to store integer values, which is then supplied to the EMA calculation. However, when passing an argument to the EMA function, a typo error occurred.

As a result, the system cannot recognize the 'length' variable because it has not been declared or used before in the script. This error likely occurred due to the typo error in the argument passed to the EMA function.

To resolve this issue, ensure that the variable names are spelled correctly and consistently used throughout the script. In this case, correcting the typo error in the argument passed to the EMA function should resolve the problem, allowing the 'length' variable to be properly recognized and utilized.

Variable is already declared: The error "Variable is already declared" occurs when a variable is declared multiple times within the same scope or when a mutable variable is re-used without the ":=" sign, which signifies assignment.

To resolve this error, you can take one of the following actions:

- Use the ":=" sign to indicate assignment for mutable variables when re-using them.
- Remove one of the variable declarations if it's redundant or unnecessary in the context.

By adhering to these guidelines, you can ensure that variables are declared and used appropriately within your script, preventing the "Variable is already declared" error.

Chapter -14: A simple cross-over strategy example

The default strategy provided by the TradingView platform for a simple moving average crossover can be accessed by clicking the "open" and then "blank strategy" tab on the Pine Script editor. This process is similar to opening a blank indicator script, as discussed earlier. The default strategy script typically includes code for implementing a basic moving average crossover strategy, which traders can then customize according to their specific requirements and trading strategies.

INPUT Default Strategy Code generated by PineScript

```
01: // This source code is subject to the terms of the Mozilla Public License 2.0
02: // © achal
03:
04: //@version=5
05: strategy("My Strategy", overlay=true, margin_long=100, margin_short=100)
06:
07: longCondition = ta.crossover(ta.sma(close, 14), ta.sma(close, 28))
08: if (longCondition)
09:     strategy.entry("My Long Entry Id", strategy.long)
10:
11: shortCondition = ta.crossunder(ta.sma(close, 14), ta.sma(close, 28))
12: if (shortCondition)
13:     strategy.entry("My Short Entry Id", strategy.short)
```

OUTPUT Default PineScript Strategy

In line no. 4, there is a comment marked with "//" followed by the script's version, which is 5 in this instance. At the time of writing this book, version 5 is the latest available version of the script.

Line no. 5 utilizes the strategy() function instead of the indicator() function, which is typically used for creating indicator scripts. The strategy function declaration at the beginning of the script informs the system that we are writing a strategy script, not an indicator script. If the system fails to find any statement to open an order, it will generate an error during compilation. The arguments for the strategy function can initially be kept simple, similar to those of the indicator function, including the title of the script and the overlay argument. All other arguments are optional and can be discussed in upcoming sections.

Line no. 7 features the ta.crossover function, which checks whether the value of the first argument has crossed over the value of the second argument. At the crossover point, the condition becomes true; otherwise, it is false. Similarly, Pine Script offers another function, ta.crossunder, which evaluates to 'true' when the value of the first argument crosses below the value of the second argument. The ta.crossunder function is utilized in the script at line no. 11.

The boolean variable longCondition becomes 'true' when the slow-moving average crosses over the long-moving average. Similarly, the shortCondition boolean variable becomes true when the short moving average crosses under the long moving average.

In any case, you can make a crossover function work as a crossunder by changing the order of arguments. For example, if shortCondition is defined as:

```
ShortCondition = ta.crossunder(ta.sma(close, 14),ta.sma(close,28))
```

It can also be written as:

```
ShortCondition = ta.crossover(ta.sma(close, 28),ta.sma(close,14))
```

The result of both conditions is the same.

On lines 9 and 13, a new function called strategy.entry is introduced. The strategy.entry function directs the system to initiate a long or short position based on its arguments. While the details of the strategy.entry function and its arguments will be discussed in forthcoming chapters, currently, it requires two mandatory arguments: the "id" of the trade and the instruction to go long or short.

Each trade is distinguished by its unique trade "id". With the trade "id", you can modify, cancel, or close the trade. This identification system proves useful when managing multiple orders within the system, facilitating easier tracking and action-taking.

The second argument of the strategy.entry function is a constant value, either strategy.long or strategy.short. As implied, it instructs the system to open a position in the specified direction. For instance, if there is an existing open position for a certain lot in one direction (e.g., buy), executing strategy.short will close the position.

In the provided example for order placement, other parameters such as lot size, limit order, stop, etc., are not included. These additional arguments of the strategy.entry function will be covered in subsequent chapters.

Summary

- The strategy code starts with function strategy() in place of indicator() as done in Indicator coding.
- The "ta.crossover" and "ta.crossunder" functions take two input series values and provide a boolean result of "true". In the crossover case, when the first argument's value is above the second argument's value, the result is "true". In the case of crossunder, vice-versa is true.
- The strategy.entry function is for opening a long or short position.
- Any trade can be identified by its trade id.

Chapter -15: Evaluating Trading Strategies

A carefully developed script, backed by thorough back-testing and live market validation, can yield a strategy with promising returns and lower risk. While there are many promising scripts available in TradingView's public library, some claiming success rates as high as 95%, it's crucial to exercise caution when relying on them.

Many factors can contribute to inconsistencies between back-testing results and live market performance. These include testing in rising markets and applying them in declining markets, as well as potential coding errors. In earlier versions of PineScript, using data from higher time frames for trading in lower time frames often yielded positive back-testing results. However, bugs present in older versions have been addressed in the latest releases.

- To select strategy scripts from the public library effectively, consider the following guidelines:
- Avoid using older version scripts; try to utilize or code them in the latest versions of PineScript.
- Independently review scripts for potential logical errors.
- Before using a script, thoroughly understand the underlying strategy, including its logic, indicators used, and entry/exit conditions.
- Conduct thorough back-testing across rising, declining, and flat markets to assess performance.
- Assess whether the strategy is suitable for current market conditions, including volatility, trends, and overall market sentiment.
- Ensure that the strategy includes robust risk management principles, such as stop-loss orders, position sizing, and risk-reward ratios.
- Leverage TradingView's community forums and discussions to gather feedback and insights from other traders who have used the script.
- Stay informed about new developments, strategies, and updates in trading methodologies and techniques to enhance your trading skills and knowledge.

Prior to implementation, test the trading strategy in a live market environment to validate its effectiveness.

By adhering to these guidelines and exercising due diligence, you can make informed decisions when selecting and utilizing trading strategy scripts from TradingView's public library..

Using Public Library for selecting a script

In previous sections, I discussed utilizing indicators from the public library. Similarly, you can access strategies shared by TradingView users by selecting them from the public library. While some strategy codes may be hidden, you have the authorization to use them on any chart of your choosing. Additionally, some codes are openly accessible with full permissions.

Now, I'll be selecting and evaluating a few strategy scripts. Prior to assessing the back-testing results of these scripts, it's important to note that they may employ varied back-testing periods, time frames, and tickers. Therefore, comparing back-testing results among these scripts isn't feasible unless they're standardized by testing them all within the same back-testing period, time frame, and asset.

To access strategy scripts, click the "fx" button located at the top of your TradingView chart page. The button's location is indicated below:

After clicking the "Indicators & Strategies" and "Public Library" buttons, you'll see a comprehensive list of all available indicators and strategies on your screen. From there, you can sort these indicators and strategies by the author's name or by the number of likes. Typically, a higher number of likes indicates a higher probability that the script is of good quality.

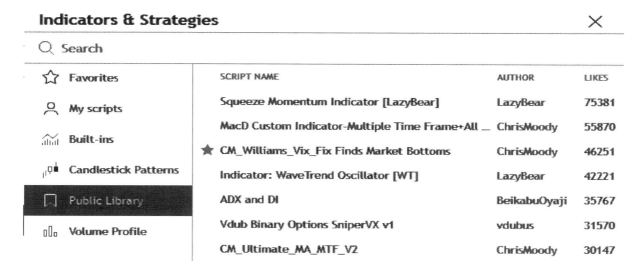

The list presents both Indicators and Strategies together, which can sometimes make it challenging to identify strategies. To help you navigate, please refer to the diagram on the following page where I've highlighted a strategy for clarity.

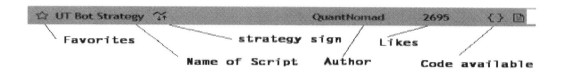

You have the option to add the script in your favourites or click them to add them to the chart. In case the script code is open, you can see the code; however, to make any changes in the code, you have to save the script.

Once you add a strategy script to the chart, you'll observe buy and sell signals appearing on the chart. To view the source code, simply click the "{ }" sign next to the strategy's name on the chart. If you wish to edit the source code, you must save the script by renaming it in your account.

Back-testing Option of TradingView

At the bottom of the TradingView advanced chart, you'll find the option for "Strategy Tester.".

Stock Screener ⌄	Text Notes	Pine Editor	Strategy Tester	Trading Panel

The Strategy Tester feature in TradingView provides values of parameters obtained after backtesting a script. Unlike Amibroker or other similar tools, in TradingView, the script itself defines the backtesting period. Below are the results obtained for the selected strategy:

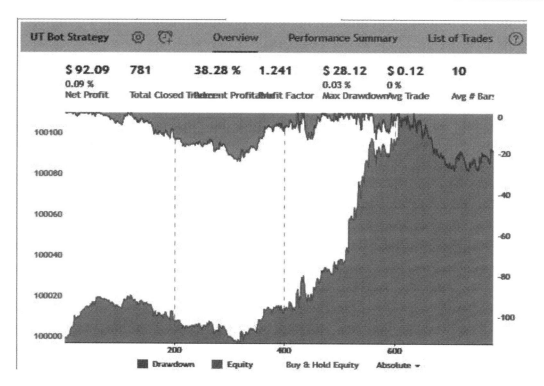

UT Bot Strategy	⚙ ⏱		Overview	Performance Summary		List of Trades	?
$ 92.09	781	38.28 %	1.241	$ 28.12	$ 0.12	10	
0.09 %				0.03 %	0 %		
Net Profit	Total Closed Trades	Percent Profitable	Profit Factor	Max Drawdown	Avg Trade	Avg # Bars	

The total profit amounts to approximately USD 92.09 after executing 781 trades, with 38.28% of the trades being profitable. Each trade was kept open for 10 bars. The strategy was initially applied to an hourly chart, and the results reflect performance within that timeframe. Upon changing the chart's time frame to daily, the corresponding results are as follows:

UT Bot Strategy	⚙ ⏱		Overview	Performance Summary		List of Trades
$ 3.36	1423	29.73 %	1.011	$ 36.74	$ 0.002	8
0 %				0.04 %	0 %	
Net Profit	Total Closed Trades	Percent Profitable	Profit Factor	Max Drawdown	Avg Trade	Avg # Bars in

Change of time frame has also changed the results, which are now poorer.

The detailed tabulated summary of results can be obtained by going to the "Performance Summary" tab available in "Strategy Tester", and the "List of Trades" are also available.

The "List of Trades" details captured trades from Feb 2018 to Oct 2021.

The performance summary tabulates many parameters; however, the major ones are here.

	All	Long	Short
Net Profit	$ 3.36 0 %	$ 73.62 0.07 %	$ -70.26 -0.07 %
Gross Profit	$ 306.88 0.31 %	$ 209.92 0.21 %	$ 96.96 0.1 %
Gross Loss	$ 303.52 0.3 %	$ 136.30 0.14 %	$ 167.22 0.17 %
Max Drawdown	$ 36.74 0.04 %		
Buy & Hold Return	$ 98993333.33 98993.33 %		

According to the table, the buy and hold strategy could have yielded a return of approximately 98993.33%, whereas our strategy only managed to achieve almost 0.00% return during the entire period under consideration. A detailed analysis of the results indicates that long trades were more successful than short trades executed by the strategy.

Regarding the strategy's logic, we cannot provide a definitive comment as it necessitates a thorough examination of the strategy code.

Major Parameters for Strategy Evaluation

Profit Factor: The Profit Factor of any trading strategy should ideally be greater than one. It serves as a measure of profit per unit of risk undertaken, calculated by dividing the profit by the loss incurred during the backtesting period. It's important to include trading commissions in this calculation. Higher values indicate better system performance.

Typically, Profit Factor values range from 1.25 to 2, with anything above 2 considered excellent. It's advisable to aim for at least a 1.25 Profit Factor and reject any strategy falling below this threshold..

Percent Profitable: The Percentage Profitable parameter represents the probability of winning a trade. It's calculated by dividing the number of trades closed in profit by the total number of trades executed during the backtesting period.

While many suggest aiming for a percentage of profitable trades greater than 50%, implying that at least half of the trades should end in profit, I hold a different perspective. With a reasonable stop loss and a higher risk-reward ratio, some trades may end in loss. However, a single successful trade can compensate for several unsuccessful ones.

Strategies designed to capture larger market moves may have a lower percentage of profitable trades. Conversely, intraday traders who rely on smaller price movements and smaller profits may aim for a higher percentage of profitable trades. For lower timeframes, prioritizing higher success rates in trades is advisable..

Average Trade Net Profit: The average trade net profit represents the net profit/loss per trade. It is expected out of the strategy that it would make the same amount of average profit in future trades undertaken through it.

Maximum Drawdown: It measures the maximum loss from a previous equity peak, i.e. largest drop in profit and loss account. This parameter should be less than the maximum risk a trader is willing to take on his total account. The maximum drawdown metric parameter should be within the limit of a trader's ability to take a risk.

Sharpe ratio: As per the definition from Wikipedia, the Sharpe ratio is a measure of the performance of an investment compared to a risk-free asset after adjusting for its risk. It is defined as the difference between the returns of the investment and the risk-free return, divided by the investment's standard deviation.

In simpler terms, every investment has risk due to its volatility, and the standard deviation can calculate this. Sharpe ratio tries to capture return over the risk associated with the asset. A Sharpe ratio of 1 is considered good, and a Sharpe ratio of 2 is considered very good. You should try to target a Sharpe ratio of more than 1.25.

Buy and Hold Return: This profit represents the potential earnings you could have garnered if you had purchased the asset at the start of the backtesting period and sold it at the end. Comparing the net profit earned during the testing period with the buy and hold strategy can offer insights into the effectiveness of a strategy. It's rare to find a strategy that consistently outperforms the Buy and Hold Strategy over a long investment period. If your strategy can capture 50% or more of the Buy and Hold return, it may be considered a favorable outcome. However, this parameter holds little significance for short-term or intraday traders.

Average bars in Trade: As the name suggests, this is an average number of bars in a trade for which the strategy remained in trade. Generally, this number should not be very high or very low. A very high number may indicate no stop or improper stop. A meagre number like 1 indicates that the trades are undertaken for a significantly smaller period, more profits could have been made, or there is a problem in coding that is closing trade once it gets opened.

Closed Trade: This is the number of trades the system has taken in the backtesting period. Generally, this number is higher for a long backtesting period and low for a smaller testing period.

You should keep an eye on this number and make sure that this is not very high. If the number is very high, you might be overtrading, and there may be a need to put some additional filters to avoid unsuccessful trades.

Common Mistakes in Strategy Evaluation

No commission: Many strategy scripts overlook commissions, assuming zero transaction costs, which can lead to an overestimation of profit. It's important to check if realistic commission fees have been factored into the strategy script, especially if you're executing a large number of trades, trading intraday, or working on smaller timeframes. The commission charges can be viewed in the "Strategy Tester" performance summary tab.

Slippages: During rapid market movements, it's common to experience slippage, where orders are filled at prices different from the expected market or ordered price. It's crucial to make realistic assumptions about these price differences when developing a strategy.

Not using Stops: Ensure that your strategy incorporates stops to safeguard your account balance against sudden adverse market conditions and to reduce maximum drawdown.

Overtrading: Overtrading poses higher risks as traders attempt to capture every market move, regardless of its significance. Employing additional filters to eliminate insignificant signals can help mitigate the risks associated with overtrading.

Selecting a Strategy from Public Library

Let's first take the above example; we have an output of the strategy for the "1Hrs" time frame chart:

Stock Screener ⌄	Text Notes	Strategy Tester	▫▫▫		— ☐

UT Bot Strategy ⚙ ⏱ ↧ Overview		Performance Summary		List of Trades ⑦
	All	**Long**	**Short**	
Net Profit	$ 92.09 0.09 %	$ 98.87 0.1 %	$ -6.78 -0.01 %	
Gross Profit	$ 473.76 0.47 %	$ 280.15 0.28 %	$ 193.61 0.19 %	
Gross Loss	$ 381.67 0.38 %	$ 181.28 0.18 %	$ 200.39 0.2 %	
Max Drawdown	$ 28.12 0.03 %			
Buy & Hold Return	$ 245112.61 245.11 %			

The net profit compared to a buy & hold strategy is significantly low. Additionally, the average profit per trade for AAPL is below the current market price. The negative results for short trades indicate that this strategy is not suitable for short selling. Moreover, the profit factor for short trades is undesirable at about 1.24.

With 781 trades executed over a period spanning from January 2018 to October 2021, which is over two and a half years, the number of trades appears to be quite substantial. This frequency suggests over-trading, especially considering that the strategy is initiating trades nearly daily on an hourly chart. Therefore, it's advisable to avoid using this script for AAPL in the "1hrs" timeframe.

Now, let's examine the results of the moving average crossover strategy discussed in this book, specifically for a five-year period on the daily timeframe.

Pair Trade	All	Long	Short
Net Profit	23027.85 23.03 %	7759.20 7.76 %	15268.65 15.27 %
Gross Profit	155102.30 155.1 %	82270.25 82.27 %	72832.05 72.83 %
Gross Loss	132074.45 132.07 %	74511.05 74.51 %	57563.40 57.56 %
Max Drawdown	20376.20 19.49 %		
Buy & Hold Return	19677.60 18.68 %		
Sharpe Ratio	0.106		
Profit Factor	1.174	1.104	1.265

The number of profitable trades for this strategy is about 23%, with a gross profit of 155%. Interestingly, the buy and hold strategy resulted in negative returns during the same period. Overall, the performance of this strategy appears decent and warrants further exploration through live testing.

However, comparing this strategy with the previous one poses challenges due to the different time periods and fund utilization. In the current script, I've utilized 100% of available funds, allowing for a direct comparison with the buy and hold strategy. In contrast, if the previous strategy only utilized 1% of the total funds, comparing it with a buy and hold strategy based on 100% fund utilization would not be justifiable.

Although this strategy demonstrates superiority on several parameters compared to the earlier one, blind comparisons without reviewing the code for stops, consistency, and testing on the same timeframe with the same back-testing period are not advisable. It's crucial to test various scripts available in PineScript's public library and familiarize yourself with testing parameters before proceeding with the coding of strategies..

Summary

- Strategies should be compared by using the same backtesting timeframe, equity and test period
- Scripts from the public library should be used after rigorous back-testing, analysis of the result, and converting to newer versions.
- No commission assumption and slippages are the significant reasons for inflated backtesting results.

Chapter- 16: Adding back-testing time-period

In the last chapter, we emphasized the importance of having a standardized timeframe and backtesting period when evaluating various equity, commodity, or forex strategies. Unlike some other platforms like Amibroker, where the backtesting period can be set externally, in Pine Script, the backtesting period is defined within the script itself.

To our initial crossover strategy default program, I have added a few code lines to backtest the strategy for a specific period. Before we move on to the code, study the below flow chart showing how this can be done.

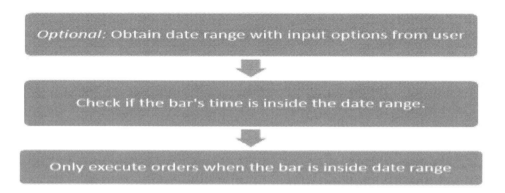

The Code

INPUT Code for crossover strategy for backtesting on a specific period

```
01: // This source code is subject to the terms of the Mozilla Public License 2.0
02: //@version=5
03:
04: strategy("tutorial- crossover", overlay=true)
05:
06: // Make input options that configure backtest date range
07: fromDay = input.int(title="Start Date",defval=1, minval=1, maxval=31)
08: fromMonth = input.int(title="Start Month",defval=1, minval=1, maxval=12)
09: fromYear = input.int(title="Start Year",defval=2015, minval=1800, maxval=2100)
```

```
10: toDay = input.int(title="End Date",defval=31, minval=1,
maxval=31)
11: toMonth = input.int(title="End Month",defval=12, minval=1,
maxval=12)
12: toYear = input.int(title="End Year",defval=2019, minval=1800,
maxval=2100)
13:
14: start    = timestamp(fromYear, fromMonth, fromDay, 00, 00)  //
backtest start window
15: finish   = timestamp(toYear, toMonth, toDay, 23, 59)      //
backtest finish window
16:
17: TimeWindow = time >= start and time <= finish
18:
19: //-----------------End of TimeWindow Code-----------------------
20:
21: longCondition = ta.crossover(ta.sma(close, 5), ta.sma(close, 10))
22: if (longCondition and TimeWindow)
23:    strategy.entry("going long", strategy.long)
24:
25: shortCondition = ta.crossunder(ta.sma(close, 5), ta.sma(close, 10))
26: if (shortCondition and TimeWindow)
27:    strategy.entry("going short", strategy.short)
28:
29: strategy.close_all(time>finish, "time up")
30:
31: plot(ta.sma(close,5),color = color.blue)
32: plot(ta.sma(close,10),color=color.red)
```

Further, a option is also provided to users to change this period as per their requirement. The input function has been used to take input from the user and is stored in the respective variables.

Explanation of Code

ANALYSIS Code for crossover strategy for backtesting on a specific period

Line no 1 is commented having the general information.

Line no 2 defines the version of the script here; in this case, the version of the script is 5

Line no 4 has a strategy function that instructs the system that the script written below is a strategy, not an indicator script. The arguments or input to the strategy function are the names of the script and overlay. In this case, the script's name is "tutorial - crossover". At the same time, the overlay value is set as "true", instructing the system to draw any label, mark or drawing on the chart itself and not below the chart. In case, the overlay is set to false, all the marking or drawing would be below the chart as it is done in the case of drawing RSI.

Line no 7 to 12 takes input from the user and store it in the respective variables. For example, in line no 7, "fromDay" is a variable; it is intended to obtain input from the user for the day from which backtesting has to be started. Since these are days from the month, the valid value for the "fromDay" variable can only be from 1 to 31.

fromDay = input.int(title="Start Date",defval=1, minval=1, maxval=31)

The input.int function allows users to provide integer input through the setting option of the strategy. This function can take many arguments; however, one argument, i.e. "defval", is compulsory. To validate data that the user inputs, we may use arguments "minval" and "maxval" to define the input's lower and upper limits, preventing user mistakes and ensuring our code works with proper values.

The value given to the title, here in the case is "Start Date", is visible to the user and provides a hint on the input type. The default value is set as 1 in the function if users do not provide any value through the setting. The value defined in the "defval" argument is used by the system in case users provide no value, which is assigned to the "fromDay" variable.

Similarly, days, months, and years for the beginning of the backtesting period and the end of the backtesting period are obtained from the user through the input function.

In the above example, we have used a new inbuilt function of pine script, i.e. timestamp. This function takes a date in "YYYY, MM, DD" format and time in hrs, mins and seconds and converts the same into a UNIX timestamp for interpretation by the system.

On lines 14 and 15, we have defined two variables, "start" and "finish", which store time in UNIX timestamp format using the timestamp function.

Now at line no 17, a boolean variable TimeWindow is defined which becomes true if the value is between the start and finish time and would become false for all time outside the start and finish. Here we have again used the inbuilt variable "time", which provides the bar's opening time. The time is compared with the value of start and finish to arrive at a value of TimeWindow.

Now, TimeWindow boolean variable is used with each "buy" or "sell" condition. In case the buy or sell conditions are 'true' and the TimeWindow condition is also 'true', the trade would be executed; else, the trade would not be executed.

On line 29, the "strategy.close_all" function is used for closing all open positions when the time is more than the finish time. This is done to include profit or loss of open positions in our strategy evaluation result.

```
strategy.close_all(condition, comment)
```

The strategy.close_all function closes all open positions when the condition defined is 'true' and shall also put remark against the trade. The function can take two arguments one is the condition for closing all the trades, and the other is a comment that has to be put against the trade in the trade log book. If you are unsure whether a position is open, it is always safe to execute strategy.close_all to close all open positions.

Line no 31 and 32 are for plotting the "Simple Moving Average" on the chart.

It is recommended that you use the above set of code with every strategy script you make. Limiting your backtesting period allows you to test your script on two different periods and compare them and also helps reduce the unnecessary burden on the shared resources of pinescript.

Summary

- A standard timeframe and fixed backtesting period are required to compare improvements made to the script or two different strategies.

- The timestamp function takes a date in "YYYY, MM, DD" format and time in hrs and seconds and converts the same into a UNIX timestamp for interpretation by the system

- The strategy.close_all function closes all the open trades when the condition becomes true.

Chapter -17: Adding Order Size and Limit Order

Before embarking on the journey of refining and improving a strategy, it's crucial to establish a standardized backtesting period, time frame, and equity for monitoring progress. To initiate this process, I aim to run my default crossover strategy, featuring the Simple Moving Average (SMA) 5 and SMA 10, for a period of five years.

The specified backtesting period will span from January 1st, 2015, to December 31st, 2019, ensuring a comprehensive evaluation of the strategy's performance over an extended timeframe. Additionally, the strategy will be executed on a daily time frame to capture broader market movements and trends effectively.

By adhering to this standardized approach, I can methodically assess the strategy's effectiveness and identify areas for improvement based on its performance within the defined parameters. This foundational step lays the groundwork for iterative optimization and refinement of the strategy to enhance its profitability and reliability over time..

The result thus obtained is as under:

$ 53.36 0.05 % Net Profit	128 Total Closed Trades	48.44 % Percent Profitable	1.87 Profit Factor	$ 11.28 0.01 % Max Drawdown	$ 0.42 0 % Avg Trade	11 Avg # Bars in

The profit provided by the script is just $53.36. In this strategy code, we took one lot per trade against the initial capital of USD 100,000, significantly reducing our profit in percentage terms.

Order Size

To maximize the utilization of available capital, we can introduce a new variable named "ordersize." This variable will represent the quantity of equity that we can purchase based on the maximum capital amount at our disposal. The calculation for determining the order size involves dividing the available funds by the price of the equity or asset. This ensures that we allocate our capital efficiently while considering the current market price of the asset.

```
ordersize = math.floor(strategy.equity/close)
```

Here, the math.floor() function serves a crucial role in converting fractional numbers to integers. In the context of purchasing equities or contracts, fractional quantities are not permissible. For instance, if the result of a calculation suggests acquiring 10.3 equities, it's not practically feasible to purchase a fraction of an equity. Therefore, the math.floor() function is employed to truncate any decimal or fractional component, ensuring that only integer quantities are considered for purchase..

Another built-in variable used in the above code for the calculation of ordersize is "strategy.equity". The strategy.equity encompasses the sum of strategy.initial_capital, strategy.netprofit, and strategy.openprofit. By dividing strategy.equity by the current closing price of the asset, the calculation aims to derive the potential quantity of equities that can be procured within the available capital. This approach ensures a judicious allocation of funds based on the prevailing market conditions and the asset's valuation at the time of execution..

Incorporating the qty=ordersize argument within the strategy.entry function is crucial to ensure the execution of trades based on the computed order size. It dictates the quantity of assets to be bought or sold in response to the trading conditions specified by the strategy. It's imperative to include this argument in both the strategy.entry functions corresponding to the longcondition and shortcondition to maintain consistency and accuracy in trade execution.

Let us see the change in the outcome.

$ 182888.32	128	48.44 %	1.817	$ 34870.96	$ 1428.81	11
182.89 %				24.05 %	1.43 %	
Net Profit	Total Closed Trades	Percent Profitable	Profit Factor	Max Drawdown	Avg Trade	Avg # Bars in

It's evident that by optimizing the strategy to utilize the maximum available capital, we've observed improvements in gross profit and max drawdown. However, it's noteworthy that the number of trades and the percentage of profitable trades have remained consistent. Despite these enhancements, the gross profit for the 5-year period amounts to approximately 182%, compared to the 324% generated by the buy and hold strategy.

Capturing around 56% of the buy and hold strategy's profit underscores the effectiveness of the optimized strategy. While the improvements are notable, it's essential to continue refining the strategy to enhance its performance further..

If you like, you can also repeat the same backtesting on "APPL" on a daily time frame for the period shown above.

Adding a Limit Order

Orders can be placed in the market in two ways:
1. **Market Order**: Market Orders are executed at the current available price at exchange. PineScript does calculations after the end of each bar; therefore, any order placed is executed at the open price of the next bar. In reality, you can seldom have a chance to purchase at the exact opening price.

2. **Limit Order**: In the case of a limit order, the order is executed when the price is equal to, or the price is better than the limit order price. In the case of long order, the better price would be less than the order price, and in the case of short order, a higher price would be considered a better price.

Example:

Order Type	Limit Price	Market Price	Order Status
Buy	100	100.1	Not Executed
Buy	100	99.9	Executed
Sell	100	100.1	Executed
Sell	100	99.9	Not Executed

In the above example for "APPL", the daily time frame backtesting, no limit order argument was used; therefore, each order was executed on the opening of the next bar after the cross-over condition was verified.

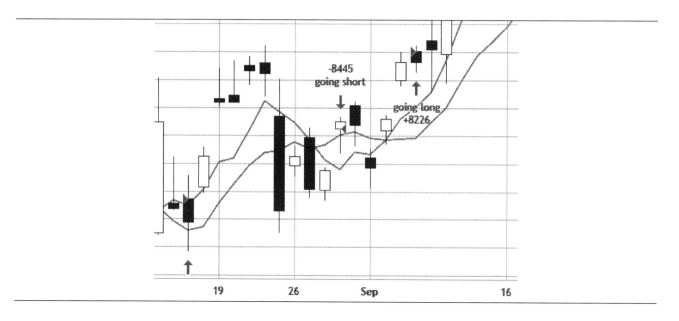

You can observe in the above chart of APPL (daily, 2019) that the order has been placed after cross-over is confirmed and on the opening price of the next candle. I want to place orders at a price equal to or less than the close of the last bar for a long order. This can be done by adding another argument, "limit," to the strategy.entry function. I am adding "limit = close" as one of the arguments for strategy.entry function, and the function now looks like this:

```
strategy.entry("going long", strategy.long,qty=ordersize,limit=close)
```

$ -2178.25	106	49.06 %	0.988	$ 37255.33	$ -20.55	13
-2.18 %				34.18 %	-0.02 %	
Net Profit	Total Closed Trades	Percent Profitable	Profit Factor	Max Drawdown	Avg Trade	Avg # Bars in

After executing the code, I have not received any encouraging results. The profit has decreased considerably, and you can also notice some unexpected trades, like the one marked below.

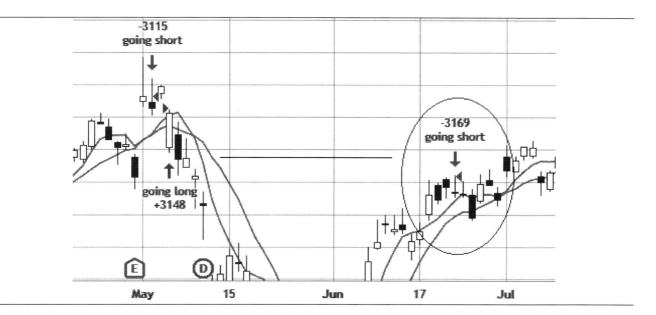

In the example above, there was an upward crossover on the first day of May, leading to the execution of a long trade on May 2/ 3. However, the price sharply declined thereafter, and despite a subsequent cross-under, the price never rose enough to close of the previous bar, thus preventing the long trade from being closed. The short order remained pending until around June 21st, when prices rebounded.

The strategy did not perform as intended due to pending orders being filled after a significant delay. Once a crossover occurred and a limit order was placed, it remained unfilled if the price did not reach the limit price. These pending orders were not cancelled, thus disrupting the strategy. In a crossover strategy that fully utilizes capital, additional orders cannot be opened if a position is already open or if orders are pending. The interference caused by pending orders resulted not only in missed opportunities but also in orders being executed at undesirable times. We will address this issue in the upcoming lessons.

Chapter – 18: Adding Stop to order

In this lecture, we will apply stop in our entry order; we have already learned to place a limit order. It becomes a market order when you don't use limit and stop argument in entry order.

If you use "limit" but no "stop" argument, it would be a limit order. i.e. the order would be executed at a price specified by the limit or at a better price than the limit price.

If you apply stop to order entry, the order would be placed once the price reaches to stop price.

If you apply both stop and limit in order entry, it would be a stop limit order. In such cases, the limit order would be placed once the price reaches to stop price. The limit price is always more than the stop price in buy orders and less than the stop price in the case of a sell order.

Type of entry order	How to make
Market order	When limit and stop arguments are not used in entry order, the order is executed on the spot market bid-ask price.
Limit order	When a limit argument is used in entry order, the order is executed if the price is equal to or better than the limit price.
Stop order	Only stop argument is used in entry order. Order is placed when the price reaches to stop price.
Stop-limit order	Both stop and limit are used in entry order. A limit order is placed when the stop price is reached.

I have tried to explain each of the above order types in the example below so you are not confused.

Understanding Stop/Limit in case of BuyOrders

Let's illustrate this with a practical example: Imagine you're watching a stock that's currently trading at $95, but you anticipate a breakout if the price rises above $100. You want to buy if the price hits $100, but you're worried about chasing the price if it moves too fast.

Without a limit, if you set your stop order at $100, as soon as the price hits $100, you'll be long in the market. However, if the price gaps up immediately after hitting $100 or there isn't enough liquidity to fill your order, you might end up with fewer shares bought at $100 and some bought at higher prices, leading to an average buying price of, say, $103. This scenario can be undesirable.

To mitigate this risk, you can use a stop-limit order. Here's how it works: You set your stop price at $100 and your limit price at $101. When the price hits $100, your limit order to buy at $101 or a better price is triggered. This means you'll only buy shares as long as the price stays below $101 or equals $101.

Type of order	Limit price	Stop Price	Current Market Price	Result
Buy	-	-	100	Executes at CMP of 100
Buy	100.1	-	100	executes as the price is better than the order price.
Buy	99.9	-	100	executes when the price would come down to 99.9 or below
Buy	-	100.1	100	executes as CMP is less than the order price, which is better than the stop price for buy.
Buy	-	99.9	100	Would wait till price reaches 99.9 for placement of order
Buy	100	99.9	-	Invalid order, a limit should be less than stop. The order would be executed at 99.9 as 99.9 is a better price than 100 to buy
Buy	99.8	99.9	100	Order not placed, waiting to place order
Buy	99.8	99.9	99.9	Limit order placed with 99.8

It may be noted that for stop orders, the system does not place an order till the price reaches to stop price. If the limit is specified after the stop, the limit order is placed, or if the limit is not specified after a stop, the order is placed at market price.

Understanding Stop/Limit in case of SellOrders

Now we take an example of limit / stop in the case when you already are long and want to save on losses or want to short.

Let us assume that you went long at 95, and now the price hovers around 101. You feel that if prices dip below 100, the market can crash, and your profit may get wiped out. To save on losses, you want to exit the market as soon as prices are below 100. In another scenario, you have information that the market would crash below 100; right now, the market is hovering around 101; you are waiting for the right time to short some stocks when the price goes below 100.

You can take stop /limit when CMP is higher than stop/limit prices in both conditions. You can use stop = 100 or below and limit below stop. Below is the table showing various options and their result.

Type of order	Limit price	Stop Price	Current Market Price	Result
Sell	-	-	100	Executed at CMP of 100
Sell	100.1	-	100	executes when the price reaches 99.9 or lower
Sell	99.9	-	100	executes as the price is better than the order price.
Sell	-	100.1	100	executes as CMP is less than the stop price.
Sell	-	99.9	100	waits till price reaches 99.9 for placement of market order
Sell	99.8	99.9	-	Invalid order, the limit should be greater than stop. Would execute at Stop price only.
Sell	99.9	99.8	100	Order not placed, waiting to place order
Sell	99.9	99.8	99.8	Limit-order placed at 99.8 with execution at 99.9.

Here is the code for adding a stop to entry order; we add another argument, "stop", to the strategy.entry. We add stop=close[1], i.e. stop equal to the "close" value of the last bar. The limit order would be placed only once the price has reached the stop. We take an example, let we want to go long and place a limit order as 101 and stop as 100, the order would be placed only once the price reaches 100 and the order is limit 101. Any price below 101 is a better price for buy-order; therefore, if the current market price is 100.4, it would get executed.

Suppose the price gap-up and opens at 101.1, the order limit would be placed by stop; however, it would only get executed once the price comes down to 101 or below. Usually, stop and limit are both used for breakout strategies where there are chances of a sudden rise in price or gap up, and we want to buy only after a breakout but before it's too late.

In the case of day frame trading, gap-ups are more frequent than intraday; we are using both limit and stop. We are putting stop=close[1]

Example Adding stop/limit entry – Buy Order

The stop price is a trigger price, i.e. a price to initiate action. Let us take a situation where the current price is 100, and I want to place an order when the price reaches 99. In such a case, I can simply place my order at 99 and wait for prices to drop to 99. Another condition is that I am waiting for a break out above 101. In such a case, if I place a buy order for 101, it would get executed at the current market price of 100.

It is desirable to use a limit only. In case the current Market Price (CMP) is lower than the price you want to place a buy order, you can use stop. I have created a small code to test stop/limit orders.

```
//-----------------End of TimeWindow Code--------------------

ordersize=floor(strategy.equity/close)

longCondition = ta.crossover(ta.sma(close, 5), ta.sma(close, 10))
plotshape(longCondition, color = color.green, style = shape.circle,
location = location.abovebar) // plot circle

strategy.entry("going long",
strategy.long,qty=ordersize,limit=close[1]-1,stop=close[1],when =
longCondition and TimeWindow)
if longCondition
    line.new(bar_index, close[1],bar_index-1,close[1], xloc = xloc.bar
_index, color=color.blue)
    line.new(bar_index, close[1]-1,bar_index-1,close[1]-1, xloc=xloc.bar
_index, color=color.blue)

//-------------plotting crossover-----------------
```

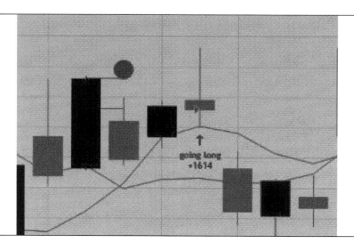

In the above code, only one entry condition has been created. Limits and stop have been plotted on the chart along with simple moving averages. For identification of crossover, a circle above the bar of crossover confirmation has been drawn. The time window function date from 1st March 2020 to 31st Dec 2020 has been used on a 1-day time frame "APPLE INC" chart. The first cross-over with successful trade execution with limit =close[1]-1 and stop=close[1] happens on 31st March 2020.

In the image, the upper line is the stop line, and the lower line represents the limit. The system identified the crossover on the red bar with a green circle.

Now let's change the limit price from close[1]-1 to close[1]+1 and see what happens. In this case, close[1] is the stop price; therefore limit buy price is more than the stop price.

Code:

```
strategy.entry("going  long",  strategy.long,  qty=ordersize,  limit=
close[1] +1,stop=close[1],when = longCondition and TimeWindow)
if longCondition
    line.new(bar_index,      close[1],bar_index-1,close[1],      xloc=xloc.
bar_index, color=color.blue)
    line.new(bar_index,   close[1]+1,bar_index-1,close[1]+1,  xloc=xloc.
bar_index, color=color.blue)
```

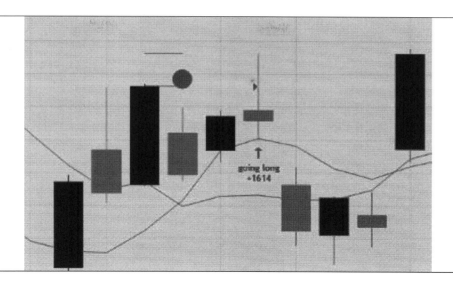

The upper line (just above the round dot) represents the limit price, and the lower line (just on the round dot) is the stop price. The trade had executed at stop price and not on limit price because the order was placed when the price reached stop price and for a buy condition better price means a lower price. Here limit was higher than the stop price, and the stop price was better, and thus the order was executed on the order price.

Example Adding stop/limit entry - Sell Order

In the case of a sell order, a better price is a price higher than the stop and limit. If the limit is higher than stop, the order would be placed on the stop but executed at the limit. However, if you put a limit price lower than the stop price, the order would be executed at the stop price.

Here is a code snippet wherein the daytime frame chart of "Apple Inc" and TimeWindow from 1st Jan 2020 to 31st Dec 2020 is used.

```
//----------------End of TimeWindow Code----------------------------

ordersize=floor(strategy.equity/close)

shortCondition = ta.crossunder(ta.sma(close, 5), ta.sma(close, 10))

plotshape(shortCondition, color = color.green, style = shape.circle,
location = location.abovebar) // plot circle

strategy.entry("going short", strategy.short,qty=ordersize, limit=
close[1]+1,stop=close[1],when = shortCondition and TimeWindow)
```

```
if shortCondition
    line.new(bar_index, close[1],bar_index-1,close[1],
xloc=xloc.bar_index, color=color.blue)
    line.new(bar_index, close[1]+1,bar_index-1,close[1]+1,
xloc=xloc.bar_index, color=color.blue)

strategy.close_all(time>finish, "time up") //close all open trade after
backtesting time ends
//--------------plotting crossover----------------
plot(ta.sma(close,5))
plot(ta.sma(close,10))
```

The code is similar to the previous code; only a short entry position has been allowed without the possibility to close the position. You can repeat this code on the "APPLE INC" day chart or any other equity for your better understanding.

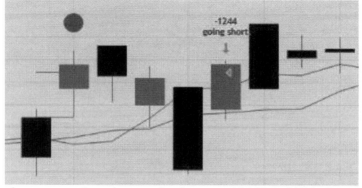

We have the chart for the transaction that took place on 11th Feb 2020. Cross-under was identified on the second candle from the left. The upper line represents the limit price, and the lower line represents the stop price. The setup had to wait for 3 days/candles before execution. On the second candle, after identification of the cross under, the price went below the stop price, and a limit order was placed. The limit order was executed on the 4th candle at the limit price after identification of cross-under.

The point to be noted is that after placing an order, the order would wait until it is modified/cancelled or filled. In the above case, after our cross-under, cross-over also took place before the order, and as such, this short order was not desirable.

Applying stop to CrossOver Strategy.

INPUT Code for crossover strategy with the stop argument

```
19: //----------------End of TimeWindow Code----------------------
```

```
20: ordersize=floor(strategy.equity/close)
21: longCondition = ta.crossover(ta.sma(close, 5), ta.sma(close, 10))
22: if (longCondition and TimeWindow)
23:   strategy.entry("going long",
strategy.long,qty=ordersize,limit=close,stop=close[1])
24:
25: shortCondition = ta.crossunder(ta.sma(close, 5), ta.sma(close, 10))
26: if (shortCondition and TimeWindow)
27:   strategy.entry("going short",
strategy.short,qty=ordersize,limit=close,stop=close[1])
28:
29: strategy.close_all(time>finish, "time up")
30:
31: plot(ta.sma(close,5),color = color.blue)
32: plot(ta.sma(close,10),color=color.red)
```

In the above code, the limit is on the current bar's close, and the stop is as per the last bar's close. In case it is 'crossover' resulting in a condition to buy, we may have the following:

1. The close of the last bar was higher than the close of the current bar
2. The close of the last bar was lower than the close of the current bar

Since crossover has taken place, it is more likely that the close of the current bar is higher than the close of the last bar resulting in a higher limit price than the stop price. Order is more likely to be executed at the last bar's close.

The result has improved, 274.82% profit in 52 trades. Overall profit per trade has also increased; however, the profitable number of trades is more or less at the same level.

$274819.72	52	44.23 %	3.482	$25520.57	$5284.99	25
274.82 %				10.55 %	5.28 %	
Net Profit	Total Count Trade Percent Profitable Profit Factor			Max Drawdown	Avg Trade	Avg # Bars in

One more argument of strategy.entry is "when". "when" takes condition for execution of strategy.entry function. If we use "when", we can safely remove the "if" condition before strategy.entry. Below is the code for a crossover with the 'when' argument.

```
21: longCondition = ta.crossover(ta.sma(close, 5), ta.sma(close, 10))
22:
23: strategy.entry("going long",
strategy.long,qty=ordersize,limit=close,stop=close[1],when=
longCondition and TimeWindow)
```

```
24:
25: shortCondition = ta.crossunder(ta.sma(close, 5), ta.sma(close, 10))
26:
27: strategy.entry("going short",
strategy.short,qty=ordersize,limit=close,stop=close[1],when=
shortCondition and TimeWindow)
28:
29: strategy.close_all(time>finish, "time up")
30:
31: plot(ta.sma(close,5),color = color.blue)
32: plot(ta.sma(close,10),color=color.red)
```

After making this change, no change would appear in the result window. This has been discussed for the sake of completeness of strategy.entry function and to make the code cleaner.

Now I am modifying my entry function as under:

```
strategy.entry("going long", strategy.long, qty=ordersize,
limit=close[1]+ta.atr(7),stop=close[1],when=longCondition and
TimeWindow)

strategy.entry("going short", strategy.short,qty=ordersize,
limit=close[1]-ta.atr(7),stop=close[1],when=shortCondition and
TimeWindow)
```

Now, observe that I have put a stop as close[1] and limit as close[1]+ta.atr(7), which would be above stop. The buy order would be placed when the price reaches close[1] for a price of close[1]+ta.atr(7). If the trend goes against, the order would not be executed, and if the trade is in favour, it would be executed.

$ 243144.43	86	47.67 %	2.152	$ 66514.15	$ 2827.26	16
243.14 %				30.66 %	2.83 %	
Net Profit	Total Closed Trades	Percent Profitable	Profit Factor	Max Drawdown	Avg Trade	Avg # Bars in

The above is a result of our revised stop and limit condition. The result has improved because the number of bars per trade has come down while profit has not come down significantly. The number of profitable trades has also increased. However, the drawdown has increased almost 3 times.

We can further use coding to drawshape for identifying crossovers as we had done in earlier examples. We can also draw stop and limit prices using plot functions for each crossover/crossunder.

I suggest you make some changes to the code provided. Use the last bar's low or high as a stop or limit.

Chapter-19: Adding Stop to Exit Trade

In this chapter, we will study a new function, "strategy.exit". It takes conditions for exiting from already taken trade. We have already coded for cross-overs, we are long, and we hold the position until we cross-under. At any point in time, we are either long or short. We have entered the trade through the function "strategy.entry". In case we are already long, and we have cross-under, the already opened long position is closed by the system.

Trade #	Type	Signal	Date	Price	Contracts	Profit
1	Entry Short	going short	2015-01-08	27.34	3658	$ 292.64 0.29 %
	Exit Short	going long	2015-01-14	27.26		
2	Entry Long	going long	2015-01-14	27.26	3600	$ -1080.00 -1.1 %
	Exit Long	going short	2015-01-20	26.96		
3	Entry Short	going short	2015-01-20	26.96	3681	$ -4711.68 -4.75 %
	Exit Short	going long	2015-01-26	28.24		

A quick review of the list of trades for the CrossOver strategy confirms that we were in trade at every point in time. The capital utilization was 100% for the entire period under backtesting. Now intending to improve upon the strategy, we want to exit when a trend starts reversing. I want to exit early in trade and reduce the utilization of funds.

For the purpose of exiting early we have two functions 1) strategy.close() and 2) strategy.exit(). In this chapter, we will focus only on strategy.exit.

Function strategy.exit

Before we discuss strategy.exit(), I want to introduce you to two more inbuilt variables, i.e. strategy.position_avg_price and strategy.position_size.

As the name suggests, the "strategy.position_avg_price" variable stores the average entry price of the currently open market position, and the "strategy.position_size" variable stores the size of the strategy's market position. When we are long, the variable "strategy.position_size" has a positive value; in the case of short, it stores a negative value.

The "strategy.exit" is re-calculated with each bar, and if already having "strategy.exit" pending, this code can modify it. The "strategy.exit" function helps us from exiting from trade without waiting for the short condition to become true. If an exit order is generated without an entry order being filled; the exit order would wait and execute after the entry order is executed.

The complete syntax of strategy.exit function is as under:

> strategy.exit (id, from_entry, qty, qty_percent, profit, limit, loss, stop, trail_price, trail_points, trail_offset, oca_name, comment, when, alert_message)

All the arguments are optional except id. If the condition for execution of strategy.exit() is not defined externally, the same has to be defined under the argument 'when'. Here we will discuss arguments that are used more frequently:

```
strategy.exit("going long", stop=strategy.position_avg_price –
ta.atr(7), when =strategy.position_size > 0)
```

Trade ID: Strategy.exit would exit which trade? Short or long? for this purpose, we have to provide a trade ID to the function; this helps identify a trade. Trade ID can be used to modify or cancel any order.

Adding Stop to CrossOver Strategy

The next argument to strategy.exit function is stop=strategy.position_avg_price-ta.atr(7). A market order would be placed to exit the long trade once the price reaches to stop price. Here, ta.atr(7) is an average true value, a measure of volatility and strategy.position_avg_price is the price at which we had opened this position.

If the prices fall below ta.atr(7), i.e. average 'true' value for 7 periods, this will close the trade. The following argument to the function strategy.exit is "when=strategy.position_size > 0"; this means that this exit order would only be placed once we are already long. Otherwise, this code might sell equity through exit order, and if we do not have equity, it will generate a short sell. In other terms, this is used to reduce the complexity of trade.

Similarly, the exit condition for the short trade has been defined:

```
strategy.exit("going short", stop=strategy.position_avg_price +
ta.atr(7), when =strategy.position_size < 0)
```

I would not explain this code, and I hope that you will be able to understand this code after the explanation provided for the exit condition for the long trade.

We would add the above two codes, save our earlier code (the last one with revised stop and limit) for the crossover strategy, and add it to the chart to obtain results.

$66594.10	92	33.7 %	1.443	$27305.95	$723.85	10
66.59 %				27.31 %	0.72 %	
Net Profit	Total Closed Trades	Percent Profitable	Profit Factor	Max Drawdown	Avg Trade	Avg # Bars In

The result has, however, reduced considerably; the profitable trades have come down to 33.7% only.

What else can be done to improve on the result? We can revise stop as we move. I made minor changes to the code for the "long" trade.

```
atrData = ta.atr(7)
stop_long = strategy.position_avg_price - atrData
if strategy.position_size > 0
        if stop_long < (close[0]-atrData)
                Stop_long:=close[0]-atrData
```

I am trying to revise the stop after the price moves in a favourable direction. Similarly, I have used code for short. I save this code, and the results are still not encouraging

$13268.53	98	38.78 %	1.117	$22313.90	$135.39	8
13.27 %				22.31 %	0.14 %	
Net Profit	Total Closed Trades	Percent Profitable	Profit Factor	Max Drawdown	Avg Trade	Avg # Bars In

Adding trail_price and offset argument to Exit function

Instead of using a bunch of code to improve my stop prices, we have another option in strategy.exit function, i.e. another argument of trail_price and trail_offset.

Trade exit stop loss would be placed when the price reaches trail_price, and this stop loss would be some points below the trailing price as defined in offset.

So say I took equity at 100, put a trailing price of 105 and offset as 2. When the price reaches 105, a stop-loss is generated at 103; if the price moves further up, this stop-loss would also increase by the same number of points. Now say the new price is 106, then the stop loss would be 2 points below at 104. Now, if the price again moves up to 107, then the new stop loss would be 105. If prices move back from this point, the stop-loss will not change, and when the stoploss price is hit, a market order would be placed to exit from the market.

The only problem is that trail_price is defined in price; however, offset is defined in terms of ticks. If the minimum tick is $0.05 and I want to put $2 of offset from trail_price, it would be 2/0.05, i.e. 40 ticks.

The pinescript also has an inbuilt variable syminfo.mintick, which provides the value of mintick for the scrip on the chart.

Now in the code, I would add two more arguments, trail-price, I would define trailing price as purchase price plus ta.atr(7) for long condition. and offset as ta.atr(7) divided by syminfo.mintick to convert it into the number of ticks.

```
strategy.exit("going long", trail_price= strategy.position_avg_price +
atr(7),trail_offset= ta.atr(7)/syminfo.mintick, when
=strategy.position_size > 0)

strategy.exit("going short",trail_price= strategy.position_avg_price -
atr(7),trail_offset= ta.atr(7)/syminfo.mintick, when
=strategy.position_size < 0)
```

$ 122054.88	101	57.43 %	1.716	$ 28810.93	$ 1208.46	7
122.05 %				13.61 %	1.21 %	
Net Profit	Total Closed Trades	Percent Profitable	Profit Factor	Max Drawdown	Avg Trade	Avg # Bars In

Here is our result using trail_price and trail_offset, profit increased to 122%, and profitable trades are 57.43%. Drawdown is lesser while the average number of bars per trade has also come down to 7.

What if I use trail_price with a stop?

Stop with trail_price in the exit function

Stoploss in trail_price is only implemented when the price reaches trailing_price, and in the absence of stop, there is no stoploss until the price reaches trailing price. Below is the code, where I have included stop and triling_price.

```
strategy.exit("going long",stop=strategy.position_avg_price - atrData,
trail_price=strategy.position_avg_price +
atr(7),trail_offset=ta.atr(7)/syminfo.mintick, when
=strategy.position_size > 0)

strategy.exit("going short",stop=strategy.position_avg_price +
atrData,trail_price=strategy.position_avg_price -
atr(7),trail_offset=ta.atr(7)/syminfo.mintick, when
=strategy.position_size < 0)
```

$ 55257.66	102	49.02 %	1.395	$ 30137.60	$ 541.74	5
55.26 %				16.61 %	0.54 %	
Net Profit	Total Closed Trades	Percent Profitable	Profit Factor	Max Drawdown	Avg Trade	Avg # Bars in

Upon execution of the above code, the result is about 55% profit with winning trade at 49%; however, bars per trade have gone down.

Why has my profit reduced after applying the best available practices of the market? The number of profitable trades has also reduced. Either entry should be made better or stop should be more. I increased my stop by taking double ta.atr(7). I save the code and execute the code.

$ 147918.85	100	58 %	1.818	$ 29832.08	$ 1479.19	7
147.92 %				13.34 %	1.48 %	
Net Profit	Total Closed Trades	Percent Profitable	Profit Factor	Max Drawdown	Avg Trade	Avg # Bars in

The result is 147% profit with 100 trades, and profitable trades are 58%.

	All	Long	Short
Net Profit	$ 147918.85 147.92 %	$ 114280.81 114.28 %	$ 33638.04 33.64 %
Gross Profit	$ 328803.54 328.8 %	$ 189385.12 189.39 %	$ 139418.42 139.42 %
Gross Loss	$ 180884.69 180.88 %	$ 75104.31 75.1 %	$ 105780.38 105.78 %
Max Drawdown	$ 29832.08 18.54 %		
Buy & Hold Return	$ 378056.89 378.06 %		
Sharpe Ratio	0.245		
Profit Factor	1.818	2.522	1.318

I think we have improved our results significantly. The average number of bars we are holding has also come down to 7.

Chapter – 20: Custom Screener

After publishing my last book, I received some requests to provide a screener code. In this chapter, we will discuss screeners. Screeners are software or tools to check many stocks from your list of stocks/forex for a particular condition. Suppose you have a strategy that requires certain conditions to be fulfilled before a trade can be taken. The condition on a single stock under your chart can come once a month; what would you do? Would you take one trade in a month? You may have to manually open each chart to find the condition, or you may be required to run a script on all such stocks individually to find your setup. The entire process could be very time-consuming, and the opportunity may be lost due to inefficient screening of all stocks.

Screening multiple stocks can at least provide you with one trade per day. TradingView also offers a screener on its home page.

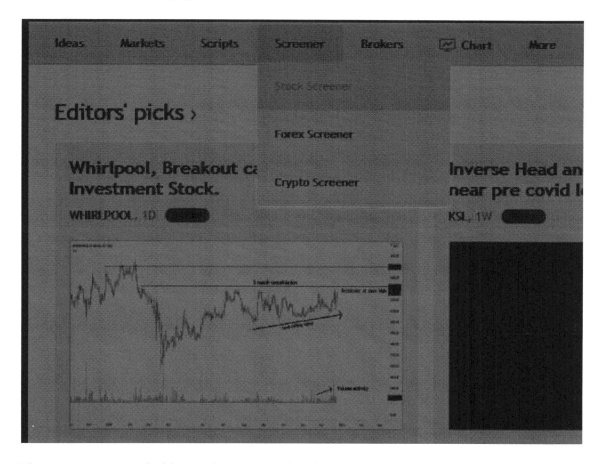

The screener provided by tradingview is fundamental and does not offer much flexibility. You can filter stocks based on fundamentals like market capitalization, the volume traded and earnings per share.

Here we also have an option for filtering stocks based on technical parameters, like moving averages, RSI, etc. However, you cannot filter based on custom parameters.

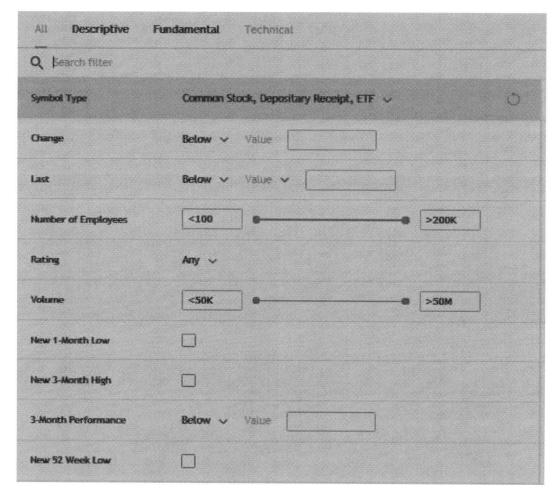

Here on your screen is a window for technical filtering of stocks. You can try them out, but you would find that they have limited functionality. You can find an EMA of 7 or 14, but you don't have the option to filter stocks based on a custom period of EMA like 8 or 9.

In this regard, I feel that the screener provided by "chartink" on another website is better.

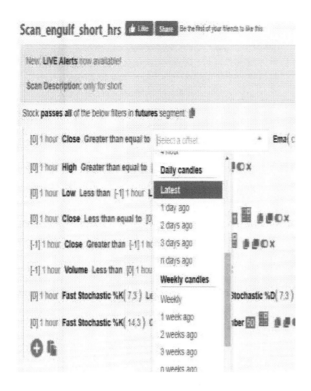

Unfortunately, this website only supports Indian exchange. Now say we want to create a custom screener to find out gap up stocks. The screener of tradingview cannot provide this functionality. Further, another site, "CHARTINK", can help only Indian traders.

Limitation of Custom screener

The pine script is not designed to do a screening job; however, looking at the need and limited capabilities of available screeners, we may need to make a custom screener in the pine script. Though we would be able to make a screener but following would be significant limitations/drawbacks:

1. The script would require a lot of code repetitions and hard work during coding.
2. Further, it would only allow simultaneously screening of 40 stocks or forex pairs.

As I told you before, TradingView does not allow excessive use of resources by one user as these resources are shared; they have put in a limitation that has resulted in screening of only 40 stocks/forex pairs at a time.

Developing Screener in PineScript

The code for the screener is straightforward. The complete code is given below. I have replicated the code for only 5 stocks, and it requires much typing and would un-necessary occupy book space. Here, you can observe that for each equity, separate codes of lines are written, resulting in a lot of code writing. You can add more stock or forex to the list by simply replacing the name of the scrip with other scrips.

INPUT Custom Screener

```
01: //@version=5
02: indicator("Gap up Screener", overlay = true)
03:
04: condition() => open > (close[1] * 1.0025)
05:
06: ACC_result = request.security('ACC', 'D', condition())
07: ADANIPORTS_result = request.security('ADANIPORTS', 'D', condition())
08: AMBUJACEM_result = request.security('AMBUJACEM', 'D', condition())
09: ASIANPAINT_result = request.security('ASIANPAINT', 'D', condition())
10: AXISBANK_result = request.security('AXISBANK', 'D', condition())
11:
12: label1 = '------GapUps -------\n'
13: label1:= ACC_result? label1+'ACC\n': label1
14: label1:= ADANIPORTS_result? label1+'ADANIPORTS\n': label1
15: label1:= AMBUJACEM_result? label1+'AMBUJACEM\n': label1
16: label1:= ASIANPAINT_result? label1+'ASIANPAINT\n': label1
17: label1:= AXISBANK_result? label1+'AXISBANK\n': label1
18:
19: caption = label.new(bar_index, close, label1,color=color.blue,
20:   textcolor=color.black,style=label.style_labeldown,
21:   yloc = yloc.price)
22: label.delete(caption[1])
```

First, we would understand the code, and then I would tell you how you can make this code with the help of the Microsoft excel function without much typing.

The first line no 2 of the code is:

indicator("Gap up Screener", overlay = true)

This line defines the name of the indicator "GAP UP SCREENER", and overlay = true is instructing the system to draw results on the chart and not below the chart.

The next line is a function is:

```
condition() => open > (close[1] * 1.0025)
```

This function would return the result in the form of 'true' and false, i.e. the result of this function would be a Boolean variable. The function will give a 'true' value if the open of the current bar is greater than the previous bar's close multiplied by 1.0025. So this function is trying to define the gap-up condition. Open of the current bar is more than the close of the previous bar. But what about this 1.0025? Why is this 1.0025 multiplied with close[1]? Well! Every time a new bar is created, it cannot always have a value equal to the previous bar's close; it could be 1-2 ticks below or above the previous bar. Does it mean that every bar is either a gap down or up? Every bar cannot be considered a gap up or down, even if it is technically and mathematically true. It should have some significant gap up or down to trade it.

We have taken a tolerance value for filtering the gap up. Only a gap up with a tolerance value of 0.25% will be reported, i.e. if the new bar is at least 0.25% above the previous close.

On line 06, we have an inbuilt function "request.security" of pinescript. The request.security function can request a data set of another symbol, resolution, or both. For example, I am working on APPLE INC 5 min timeframe, and for some purpose, I need data of APPLE INC from the day time frame, I can use request.security function.

Or say I am working on APPLE INC 5 min Time frame and I need data for GOOGL for a day time frame, Request.security function can provide me with that data.

However, this "request.security" function can be called only 40 times in a pine script. This has been done to avoid excessive resource hunting from the server. Several scripts asking data for several scripts can slow down the server, so the owners of trading view have put this limit allowing fair uses of the function and making resources equally available to all the users.

The function has been used here; the code is

```
06: ACC_result = request.security('ACC', 'D', condition())
```

To request data for a particular stock, you have to put the symbol code of the stock or forex as a string as the first input to the request.security function. Here, 'ACC" is a symbol code for a cement-producing company in India. The second input is the timeframe (resolution) for which you need data; here, I have put 'D", which means I have requested day time frame data. If you require data for another time frame, you may request data using request.security function. Available resolution from pinescript are seconds (1S, 5S, 15S, 30S), minutes (from 1 to 1440), days (from 1D to 365D), weeks (from 1W to 52W) and months(from 1M to 12M).

It is clear that I want day time frame data from ACC, but what data? I can ask for high, low, close, or volume. But I want to check the gap-up condition; I would require close and open data. If I request both the data by using a request.security function, I would have to make two different codes:

```
ACC_close = request.security('ACC', 'D', close[1])
ACC_open = request.security('ACC', 'D', open)
ACC_GapUp = ACC_open – (ACC_close** 1.0025)
```

The following are drawbacks of this method:
1. This would increase coding work; code would become lengthy
2. The limit of 40 "request.security" function calls would allow screening of 20 scrips.

I would only be able to screen 20 stocks because of the upper limit of a call to request.security function per script is 40. Therefore, the way around is to ask for results directly, i.e. open > close[1] plus tolerance from the "request.security" function, instead of individual open and close values. I have used function condition() in the "request.security" call. This would help us to have only one call per stock or forex pair to get gap information, and now I can screen 40 stocks.

Other lines of code till line 12 are the repetition of code to get data for other scripts. Now consider lines 12 and 13:

```
12: label1 = '------GapUps -------\n'
13: label1:= ACC_result? label1+'ACC\n': label1
```

On line no 12, the label1 is not an inbuilt variable or function, and making it equal to '--------GapUps--------\n' has generated a string variable. The string variable is a variable that stores alphanumeric values, and no arithmetic operations can be done on them, for example, your name. The string values are always defined within quotes.

If you people do not have prior programming experience, you would probably not be able to understand what is '\n'. In computer terms, the '\n' is equivalent to your keyboard's 'enter key'. All other strings written after '\n' would come on the next line.

On line 13, variable lable1 is already declared; and a new value is being assigned using the ':=" sign informing that this variable is mutable and the value can be changed. if 'ACC_result' is true, the value of "label1" would become label1 + 'ACC\n'; else "label1" value would be equal to "label1",i.e. no change. This means that on a gap-up condition for the scrip being true, the label value would add the name of the scrip in its list; else, there would be no addition.

The code has been repeated for all the scrips. Now, consider the below code:

```
19: caption = label.new(bar_index, close, label1,color=color.blue,
```

```
20:  textcolor=color.black,style=label.style_labeldown,
21:  yloc = yloc.price)
22: label.delete(caption[1])
```

The code on line no 19 extends to another line; it continues on lines 20 and 21. The code would generate a label on the chart showing data stored in label1 created through the previous code. However, this label has been given a name, i.e. caption.

The line label.delete(caption[1]) would delete the previously created caption. This is done for the following reasons.
1. The maximum number of labels drawn on the chart is limited.
2. Printing labels at each close of the bar would make the chart clumsy.

Here I would not discuss how the label.new function has been used as the same has already been discussed in my last book.

Below is the result after saving the code and adding it to any chart.

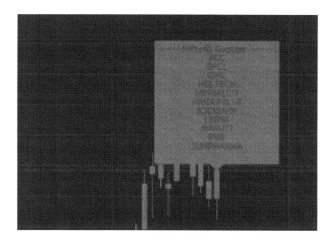

I added 40 stocks, and the results of all scrips showing gap-up are shown in the above image. The previous label was since deleted, it is not available for viewing. The next day this label would also get deleted.

Since the script only allows you to scan 40 scrips simultaneously, you can make 2-3 such scripts to cover your entire watchlist and run them on any chart to get your screener result. This would help to reduce a lot of screening work; now, instead of opening each scrip to check some conditions, you can run 2-3 scripts of pinescript.

The code we just discussed can be reused by changing the name of the scrips and adding a few more. The condition function can also be changed to suit your requirement.

Shortcut to write this big code

This code can be written and replicated as often as you want by using Microsoft excel. Microsoft Excel would save time in typing a line for each scrip.

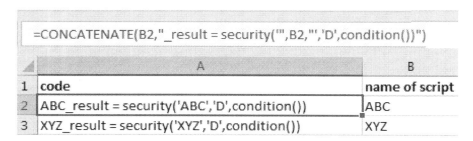

As shown above, you can use the inbuilt function CONCATENATE of excel to join various strings together.

Here in the case, the first string is 'ABC', which is in cell B1
the second string is "_result = request.security('", the string has been enclosed in quotation marks (")
The third string is again cell B1
The fourth string is ",'D',condition())"

A comma has separated all the strings in the function.
Once you have made the above in excel, you can write the name of all scrips in column B and code the code to all cells in column A and your code will be ready to use.

Now you can select your code from column A and copy-paste it to either notepad or pinescript editor.

This is a handy trick to replicate codes I often use to save time and reduce the probability of error while re-typing them multiple times.

Chapter-21: Pair-Trading Strategy

As the name suggests, you need two closely related stocks for pair trading. Both the stocks should be from the same sector, or one can be index.

The underlying principle is that the stock should move together as both are from the same sector. If any stock diverges, we assume it shall fall in line with another stock, and a trading opportunity arises.

If you are familiar with the strategy, skip the next section and continue to understand the code. If you are unfamiliar with the strategy and have never read it before, I will explain it in detail in the next section.

Selection of Pair

In pair trading, we need at least two stocks for trading purposes. We generally select equities of companies from the same sector with similar structures and activities. In pair trading, it is assumed that both the equities shall closely follow each other, and any deviation is treated as an opportunity.

For example, we have to select two stocks; I can choose two stocks from the Automobile sector or both from I.T. Sector. Further, if the nature of activities is also similar, I can safely assume that these two shall be following closely to each other. However, in mathematics, you are not allowed to assume, you can take the correlation of prices of these two equities, and if the coefficient of correlation is more significant than 0.75, they are closely linked.

Thankfully, we have a formula in excel to calculate the coefficient of correlation. In the pine script, it can be calculated by the inbuilt function "correlation". The syntax for a correlation function is as under

coefficient =correlation(x, y, length)

In the above function, all three inputs are compulsory. Both x and y are time-series values, and length is the lookback period.

It could be close of equity 1 and 2, or they can be returned per day for equity 1 and 2. even if you switch the position of x and y, the result would be the same. The length is integer input which is the lookback period for calculating correlation.

Parameters of Pair

For trading purposes following are measure parameters that can be used for pair trading. The basic assumption is that the prices, if deviated, shall converge (return) to the average values of these parameters.

Spread: Spread is the difference between daily returns.

Date	Equity A	daily return	Equity B	Daily return	spread
20180101	565.5		372		
20180102	559.5	-0.066	371.7	-0.081	0.014
20180103	560.45	-0.970	369.05	-0.713	-0.257
20180104	559.9	0.322	367.4	-0.447	0.769
20180105	563.25	-1.391	364.8	-0.708	-0.684
20180108	565.45	-1.045	357.2	-2.083	1.039

If equity A has increased by 1%, it is assumed that equity B shall also increase, but how much it would increase cannot be predicted. The only thing that can be assumed is that they shall move in the same direction. If any one of the equity does deviate from the mean of the spread, we would not be in a position to conclude; therefore, we can buy one and sell another.

The difference in prices: As the name suggests, it is a difference between the prices of two selected equities from the same sector.

Date	Equity A	Equity B	Difference
20180101	565.5	372	193.50
20180102	559.5	371.7	187.80
20180103	560.45	369.05	191.40
20180104	559.9	367.4	192.50
20180105	563.25	364.8	198.45
20180108	565.45	357.2	208.25

Similar to spread, the price difference can also return to the mean after some deviation. On this assumption, one equity can be purchased, and another can be sold.

Ratio: Ratio measure of ratios between the prices of two selected equities.

Date	Equity A	Equity B	ratio
20180101	565.5	372	1.520
20180102	559.5	371.7	1.505
20180103	560.45	369.05	1.519

20180104	559.9	367.4	1.524
20180105	563.25	364.8	1.544
20180108	565.45	357.2	1.583

The ratio is an interesting parameter, it is assumed that the ratio of these two equities shall somewhat remain constant, and any deviation from the mean shall be deemed as variation, and position can be taken.

Out of the three measures, anyone can be used for making your strategy for pair trading. However, in this course, I am taking ratios for making our pair trading strategy because it is not only easy to understand but straightforward to use and implement. Further, ratio parameters, unlike differences between prices or spreads, are reasonably stable over long periods.

Statistical Measures

The primary statistical measures are mean(average), mode, median, and standard deviation. For an understanding of any dataset, the above parameters are required. However, here we would only be using mean and standard deviation measures.

Mean is nothing but average, and we already have the "ta.sma" function in pinescript for the calculation of average. Standard deviation is a measure of volatility, which can be measured by the pinescript inbuilt function "stdev". The syntax of "stdev" is as under:

result = stdev(DataSeries, length)

Here DataSeries is the input on which we calculate standard deviation, and length is the lookback period up to which input data is to be used to calculate the standard deviation.

Meaning of Statistical Measures

Mean is the value about which other data hovers. Most of the data could be found around the mean value. In case of a data series deviation, it is assumed that the data would come back nearer to the mean value in the future.

Standard deviation is a measure of volatility. In simpler terms, it is a measure of data dispersing. In statistics, it is assumed that most of the dispersed data follow 'normal distribution' and data beyond "mean + SD" could only be about 32%, and 68% would remain inside the "mean+SD" value. Similarly, for the "mean + 2 SD", only 5% of data could be outside, and 95% of data would remain inside the "mean + 2 SD". Below is the table which gives you an idea of data dispersed about a mean value.

Value	% data sets to remain inside the value	% data sets to remain outside the value
Mean + SD	68%	32%
Mean + 2 X SD	95%	5%
Mean + 3 X SD	99.7%	0.3%

So, say we have a mean ratio of 1 and SD as 0.1, then

Measure	Value
Mean − 3 X SD	0.7
Mean - 2 X SD	0.8
Mean − SD	0.9
Mean	1
Mean + SD	1.1
Mean + 2 X SD	1.2
Mean + 3 X SD	1.3

If the present ratio value is 1.24, it can safely be assumed that there is only a 5% chance of this value increasing beyond 1.2 and a 95% chance that it would fall back to the mean value in the near future.

Similarly, if the ratio of the two equity is less than 0.8, we can assume that it is one of its extreme values, and there is a 95% chance that the value of the ratio would come back to mean.

Taking a trade

We have studied many new parameters and concepts that non-mathematical professionals could find difficult. Here, I am taking a quick recap and again explain only those parameters needed for this coding.

Step -1

Pair trading requires a pair of 2 equities. You have two options:

1. Select any two equities that have a correlation coefficient greater than 0.75. The closer the value is toward 1, they are more correlated, which means in case one equity moves in one direction. The second would also follow; otherwise, the previously moved equity would fall back.

2. Select any two equities of the same sector with similar capsize and activities. This would be through your intuition. Mostly the traders follow the second method — i.e. selection of equities by intuition.

Second Step

The mean of ratio's of prices of two equities is calculated

Third Step

Standard Deviation is calculated for the ratio of prices for some lookback period.

Entry and Exit conditions

If the current ratio of prices is above the mean plus twice the standard deviation, it is abnormally high, and there is a 95% chance of falling ratio to the mean level.

If the current ratio of prices is below the mean minus twice the standard deviation, it is abnormally low, and there is a 95% chance for rising in the ratio to the mean level.

Assuming ratio as an asset, we can buy the asset when they are abnormally low and sell the ratio when they are abnormally high.

The ratio is in the form of equity A / Equity B. A buying ratio means to buy equity A and sell equity B. In the case of selling of ratio means to sell equity A and buy equity B.

How much should be brought of one equity in comparison to other equity? Say the ratio of A to B is 1.5, for each unit of B, 1.5 units of A should be transacted.

Two equities are traded because we are assuming ratios as an asset class. We can never know whether equity A has deviated or equity B has deviated, but there would be a 95% chance that anyone has deviated. We, therefore, take trade in both the equities. Most of the time, you would observe that return is obtained from only one equity, while other provide a very low or negative return. Overall taking both the equity, you would be getting a positive return.

The code

The code for pair trading is given below:

INPUT Pair Trading

```
01: //@version=5
02: strategy("Pair Trade", overlay=false)
03: //take input from a user; I have taken 21
04: length = input(21, "Look back Period", input.integer)
05:
06: //import script data from the server, both are equities from
Exchange
07: y = log(request.security((input("TVSMOTOR")), timeframe.period,
close))
08: x = log(request.security((input("MARUTI")), timeframe.period,
close))
```

```
09: r = y/x //calculated ratio of the two values
10:
11: r_ = ta.sma(r,length) //mean value of ratio
12:
13: mr = ta.stdev(r, length) // SD of ratio
14: c = ta.correlation(x, y, length) //correlation between X and Y
15:
16: //### uncomment below block to print value of Correlation
###//
17: //c_string = tostring(c)
18: //caption = label.new(bar_index,close,c_string,color=color.blue,
19: //  textcolor=color.black,style=label.style_labeldown,
20: //  yloc = yloc.price)
21: //label.delete(caption[1])
22: //### End to print value of Correlation ###//
23:
24:
25: //buy trigger = mean - 2 std
26: buy_sl = r_ - (2.25 * mr) //buy stoploss value
27: buy_t = r_ - (2*mr) //buy trigger value
28: buy_s = r_ - mr // take profit value
29:
30: //sell trigger = mean + 2 std
31: sell_sl = r_ + (2.25 * mr) //buy stoploss value
32: sell_t = r_ + (2*mr) //buy trigger value
33: sell_s = r_ + mr // take profit value
34:
35: //plot all key variables for visual examination//
36: plot(r, color=color.white)
37: plot(buy_t, color=color.green,linewidth = 2)
38: plot(r_, color=color.blue)
39: plot(sell_t, color=color.red,linewidth = 2)
40: plot(buy_s, color=color.green,style=plot.style_linebr)
41: plot(sell_s, color=color.red,style=plot.style_linebr)
42: //End to plotting block
43:
44: ordersize=floor(strategy.equity/close) //ordersize is order qty
45:
46: strategy.entry("SE", strategy.short,qty=ordersize, when=r> sell_t)
47: strategy.close("SE", when = r < sell_s or ta.crossover(r,sell_t))
48: strategy.entry("LE", strategy.long,qty=ordersize, when=r<buy_t)
49: strategy.close("LE", when= r > buy_s or ta.crossunder(r,buy_t))
```

Explanation to code

Line 04 takes input for length and the lookback period. Depending on the timeframe and equities, this look-back period may need to be adjusted. This may require optimization manually.

Line 7 & 8 imports 'close' data for selected equities from the server through the request.security function. We have already discussed the request.security function in detail in the last chapter. In this code, an inbuilt variable timeframe.period is used. The timeframe.period is the selected time frame on the chart.

On line no 09. the "r" is a ratio between the close prices of equities, and on line 11, the "r_" is a moving average of the ratio. This is the mean value that we expect to be respected by prices upon deviation.

The "mr" variable is a standard deviation of "r" variable for the lookback period equal to length.

In line no 14, we have calculated the correlation between close prices of both the equity by taking data for the lookback period equal to "length", and the result is stored in the "c" variable.

From line no 16 to line no 22, we have code to print a label containing a value of the correlation between two equities. I have commented on the entire block. If you want to display the correlation value for your understanding, you may like to uncomment the block. We have already studied this block of code in the last chapter.

From lines 25 to 33, we have defined buy and sell triggers, equivalent to mean +/- 2 X standard deviation. We have also defined take profit and stop loss in terms of mean and standard deviations.

We have taken a conservative approach and have tried to book profit when the ratio reaches "mean + SD" for short and "mean – SD" in case of the long. Stop losses have been kept 0.25 of SD away from the entry point.

From lines 35 to 42, all the key variables have been plotted for visual examination and better understanding.

Line no 44 is ordersize which has been discussed previously also. From lines 46 to 49 are entry and exit conditions for the strategy.

Result of Pair Trading

Below is the result for 1 hrs time frame for approx 3 years of data for the selected pair. Here, the script has been run on TVS Motors only and not on MARUTI. This thus represents half of the trade.

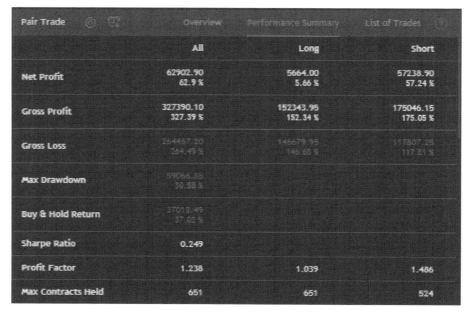

This result is more than the "buy and hold" strategy, which is about -37% during the same period (9th Jan 2018 to 9th Jan 2021). The detailed parameters of the results are presented below:

Pair Trade	All	Long	Short
Net Profit	62902.90 62.9 %	5664.00 5.66 %	57238.90 57.24 %
Gross Profit	327390.10 327.39 %	152343.95 152.34 %	175046.15 175.05 %
Gross Loss	264487.20 264.49 %	146679.95 146.68 %	117807.25 117.81 %
Max Drawdown	59066.85 26.58 %		
Buy & Hold Return	37018.49 37.02 %		
Sharpe Ratio	0.249		
Profit Factor	1.238	1.039	1.486
Max Contracts Held	651	651	524

Now the results for MARUTI, the other equity for the same period, are as under:

Again the results are better than the "buy and hold" strategy, which is -18.68%. The details of the result parameters are shown below.

Pair Trade		All	Long	Short
Net Profit		23027.85	7759.20	15268.65
		23.03 %	7.76 %	15.27 %
Gross Profit		155102.30	82270.25	72832.05
		155.1 %	82.27 %	72.83 %
Gross Loss		132074.45	74511.05	57563.40
		132.07 %	74.51 %	57.56 %
Max Drawdown		20376.20		
		19.49 %		
Buy & Hold Return		18677.60		
		18.68 %		
Sharpe Ratio		0.106		
Profit Factor		1.174	1.104	1.265

The results would vary depending on the time frame; however, overall, the strategy is profitable and requires further refining to improve upon.

Future Scope

I have provided you with a basic structure of code, wherein entry and exit conditions have been defined. The code can be modified using stop loss conditions, limit conditions, and take profit conditions.

You can also use filters like volatility, RSI, etc., for refining your entry or exit. You can also use other parameters of paired equities like spread and price differences to refine your entry strategy. The variable lookback period can be changed and optimized for different pairs.

Chapter -22: Array

The array was recently introduced by the end of 2020 in pinescript. If you already have experience in programming, you must know array datatypes. For beginners, we have added the below section to provide an understanding of the array.

We have already understood that pinescript is creating series variables and users had few choices for data storage for future use. Suppose, during the data analysis, we found that a new resistance has developed or a previously made resistance has been broken. We want to use or store this information for future trades. Traditionally, we were required to maintain the number of variables to store values of such resistances. Now with the introduction of arrays, the same can be used for storing values of various types for future use. Upon finding a new resistance, the same can be added to the list of resistances and, upon breach, can be removed from the list of resistances. By use of a list for storage of user-defined data, pinescript has opened up new opportunities for programmers in Pine Script.

Meaning of Array

An array is a special datatype in pinescript; it is a one-dimensional list in PineScript. An array can be assumed as a list of items of the same type. For example, you want to invite guests to your birthday party and make a list. This list of guests can be thought of as an array.

In array, you have the right to add anything to the list or to remove something from the list. An example is a list of guests for my birthday party.

S.no.	Name of Guest
0	Ammie
1	Ariana
2	Stephan
3	Joy
4	Maggie

Now say you want to store entire data in an array in pinescript, then you can do the same by creating an array. Let's say we create an array with the name "guest" and store this data in the array then the serial number would start from 0 to 4. For more clarity, note that for the above guest list, the array size would be 5, but the maximum serial number would be 4 because serial numbers start from 0.

You can add more names of guests either at the location zero (through a function array.unshift()) or at the end of the array, i.e. below the name of Maggie (through a function array.push()) or at any location in between array serial no 0 to 4 (through a function array.insert()). Similarly, the first name can be removed by the function array.shift(), and the last name Maggie can be removed by the function array.pop(), any name in between can be removed by function array.remove() or entire array can be cleared by function array.clear(). The syntax of the array in pinescript is similar to python. We will take examples of each of the above functions in upcoming sections.

Basics of Array

Arrays can be declared in many ways. The most common and preferred way to declare an array is shown below.

var guest = array.new_string(5)

The "var" keyword is used before the "guest" variable name to inform the system that this array will be initialized only once during the entire run. The guest array will be initialised on new bar formation if the "var" keyword is not provided before the variable "guest" name.

Now the array.new_string(5) creates an array of string datatype. This means that it can store values which are string by datatype. The total number of data it can store is five with serial no 0 to 4.

The above command has just created the variable; the values in the variables have not been initialized. You can assume that this command has only allocated memory to the variable guest for storing 5 strings.

If the command var guest = array.new_string(5,"text") is issued, it would create five strings with an initial value as "text". As shown below:

Array s.no.	Value
0	Text
1	Text
2	Text
3	Text
4	Text

I can change the value by using set commands as:
array.set(guest,0,"Ammie")
array.set(guest,1,"Ariana")
array.set(guest,2,"Stephan")
array.set(guest,3,"Joy")
array.set(guest,4,"Maggie")

The above command would make our desired list of guests. The array.set is a function that takes three arguments. The first is the name of an array variable, the second is the index of the array to which we wish to store our data, and the third is the data we wish to store. Please note that the index starts from 0 and ends at one short of array length. i.e. array.size(guest)-1

The array.size is a function that takes the array variable as an argument and provides the array size as an integer value. We will be using this function more often in upcoming examples.
Another method for declaring an array is

string[] guest = na

The above would create guest as an array of string datatype with zero size. The other data types of an array that can be created are bool, color, int, float, line, label, and string. The command would be similar to the command we just used to create a string array. An example is shown below:

Rainfall = array.new_float(5)
myColor = array.new_color(0)

If you are unsure about the size of the array you want to create, let it be of size zero. The size would be dynamic as elements are added or removed from the array. The maximum size of array allowed by pine script is 100000. This is a considerable number, and practically it should serve most of your requirements.

Adding to Array

Now, say after making a list, you want to add the name "Emma" to the list. You have three options to add this name to the list - in the beginning, at the end or in between.
Array provides us with three options for adding the name to the list.
1. **array.push(array,value)**
    Add at the bottom of the list, i.e. after the name of Maggie. You may issue a command array.push(guest,"Emma"). This command would add Emma at the bottom of the list. After adding this name to the list array.size(guest) would return 6. This means that the size of an array would increase.

2. **array.unshift(array,value)**
    Add at the beginning of the list, i.e. before the name of Ammie. You may issue a command array.unshift(guest,"Emma").

3. **array.insert(array, index, value)**
    Add in between the first and last name, say after the name of "Ariana," i.e. at array index no. 2

You may issue a command array.insert(guest,2,"Emma"). The newly added element, "Emma", would have array index no. 2.

Removing from Array

Similar to the option for adding an element to the array, we have functions for removing an element from the array - from the bottom, from the top, or between. The options available for removing elements from the array are:

1. **array.shift(array)**

   This function can remove the first name from the list. The function only requires one argument, i.e. name of the array and the first element is removed. If on the list of guests created in the section, when this command is issued, array.shift(guest), the name of "ammie" would be removed from the list.

2. **array.pop(array)**

   Similar to the array.shift function, this function also takes only one argument and removes the last name from the list. If this command, array.pop(guest), is issued to the list of 5 guests we made in section one, the name of "Maggie" would be removed by executing this function.

3. **array.remove(array,index)**

   With the above function, any array element in between the first and last element can be removed. If on the list of 5 guests we just created in section one, we want to remove the name of "Joy" at index no. 3, then we can use the function as array.remove(guest,5) to remove the name of Joy. The size of the array would get reduced.

4. **array.clear(array)**

   As the function name suggests, this function can clear all the array elements, making it empty. i.e. with zero size. This can be done by calling the function as array.clear(guest)

Reading from Array

We have read about the functions used to create an array, writing or altering values by adding or removing elements from the array. Now in this section, we will try to read from the array.

Before we move ahead, I want to let you know that each array element is not a single element but a series of elements. To make my point clearer, take the below example.

Bar-1	Bar-2	Bar-3	Bar-4	Bar-5
Ammie	Ammie	Ariana	Ariana	Ariana
Ariana	Ariana	Stephan	Stephan	Stephan

Stephan	Stephan	Joy	Joy	Joy
Joy	Joy	Maggie	Maggie	Maggie
Maggie	Maggie			

With the "var" keyword, the list is created and initialized once for each bar. Let's say bar-1 is my first bar and bar-5 is my last bar, and during one of the operations in bar no 3, I removed the first name "Ammie" from the list, reducing the array size to 4. Now, if I want to get the element at s.no. zero. The output would be a series like:

Bar-1	Bar-2	Bar-3	Bar-4	Bar-5
Ammie	Ammie	Ariana	Ariana	Ariana

The function to obtain a series of elements of any array index is array.get(array,index). So say I want to get an element at index no 2 from the array guest list as shown in the table, I can use the command as array.get(guest,2), and the result would be a series as under:

Bar-1	Bar-2	Bar-3	Bar-4	Bar-5
Stephan	Stephan	Joy	Joy	Joy

More functions on Array

The array has many other functions to assist us in working with an array. This section will discuss some more essential functions that array support. In case of any confusion or you want to learn more functions on the array, you can always refer pinescript manual available online. This book will discuss the array's most basic and frequently used functions.

We again continue with our previous example of the guest list for the five bars discussed in the above section.

Now say we want to do some operation with Stephan; for that, we need the index id of Stephan from the guest list. Index id of any value can be obtained by using the function. Now say we forget the index of Stephan, we can obtain the index of Stephan as under:

IndexNo = array.indexof(guest,"Stephan")

The above would store value 2 in the IndexNo variable for bar-1. These functions take the array's name and the element's value as input and output in a series of integers. That means it would search Stephan in all lists for each bar. The result would thus be a series as under:

Bar-1	Bar-2	Bar-3	Bar-4	Bar-5
2	2	1	1	1

If the name Stephan appears more than once in the list, then the index of the first occurrence would be reported. In case of multiple occurrences of the name in the list, we may also use the function array.lastindexof(array, value) to obtain the index of the last occurrence of the element.

Other important functions that may be used with numeric types are array.avg(), array.min(), array.max(), array.median(), array.mode(), array.standardize(), array.stdev(), array.sum(), array.variance(), array.covariance(), array.range().

Example using an array (breakout marking)

Here we are taking an example to mark a breakout of the previous pivot high or low points. To evaluate breakout, knowing the values of previous pivot highs is necessary. It is challenging to carry forward such information from bar to bar without an array. Further, in this script, an attempt is made to remove all such pivot highs or lows whose value has been breached.

Pivot high and low have been marked using an inbuilt function of pinescript, and on breakout of pivots, the same have been marked using coloured circles. Just go through the code and look at the output generated.

`INPUT` Marking Break Out

```
01: //@version=5
02: indicator("Tutorial-Breakout", overlay=true)
03: ///code for Recent Pivot Point///
04: leftBars  = input.int(4)
05: rightBars = input.int(2)
06:
07: swh = ta.pivothigh(leftBars, rightBars)
08: swl = ta.pivotlow(leftBars, rightBars)
09:
10: swh_cond = not na(swh)
11: swl_cond = not na(swl)
12:
13: plotshape(swh_cond, text = "PH", color = color.green, style = shape.arrowdown, location =
14:   location.abovebar, offset = -rightBars)
15:
16: plotshape(swl_cond, text = "PL", color = color.red,   style = shape.arrowup,   location =
17:   location.belowbar, offset = -rightBars)
18: //----------------pivot drawing ended------------------------
19: //----------------find and store pivot high and low ----------
20: var PH = array.new_float(1)
```

```
21: var PL = array.new_float(1)
22:
23: if (not na(swh))
24:    array.unshift(PH, swh)
25:
26: if (not na(swl))
27:    array.unshift(PL, swl)
28: //----------------find breakout-----------
29: for i=0 to array.size(PH)-1
30:    if close > array.get(PH,i)
31:       array.set(PH,i,10000)
32:       label1 = label.new(bar_index, low, text="", style=label.style_circle,size=size.tiny)
33:
34: for i=0 to array.size(PL)-1
35:    if close < array.get(PL,i)
36:       array.set(PL,i,0)
37:       label1 = label.new(bar_index, high, text="",color=color.red,
38:        style=label.style_circle,size=size.tiny)
39:
40: if array.indexof(PH,10000) > 0
41:    array.remove(PH,array.indexof(PH,10000))
42:
43: if array.indexof(PL,0) > 0
44:    array.remove(PL,array.indexof(PL,0))
```

OUTPUT Marking of BreakOut

The output is on the next page for the code provided above. The code marks breakout by drawing a solid circle below the bar when a pivot-high value is breached, and the next bar's close is above the pivot point.

In the case of pivot low, a solid circle is marked above the bar when a pivot low is breached, i.e., the next bar's close is below the pivot-low point.

BreakOut Code

Line 1 to 3 does not require any explanation as the same has been discussed many times in this book.

```
04: leftBars  = input(4)
05: rightBars = input(2)
06:
07: swh = pivothigh(leftBars, rightBars)
08: swl = pivotlow(leftBars, rightBars)
09:
10: swh_cond = not na(swh)
11: swl_cond = not na(swl)
```

The code in lines 4 to 11 has already been discussed in previous chapters wherein we had used them to obtain the values of pivot high & low and stored them in swh and swl variables. In case there is no pivot high/low in a particular bar value, "na" is stored in swh and swl variables.

The condition variables swh_cond and swl_cond become true if the value of swh or swl is not "na". In simpler terms, the swh_cond and swl_cond become 'true' when the bar has a pivot high/low.

Line 13 to 17 codes mark pivot high and pivot low by drawing text "PH" and "PL" on the chart. For more details on how this code works, refer to chapter 10 on "Examples on joining pivot points".

```
20: var PH = array.new_float(1)
21: var PL = array.new_float(1)
22:
23: if (not na(swh))
24:    array.unshift(PH, swh)
25:
26: if (not na(swl))
27:    array.unshift(PL, swl)
```

On lines 20 and 21, two new array variables have been defined as a float with size =1. These variables have been defined with a keyword var, meaning they would be created only upon execution for the first bar and would not be created fresh each time upon each new bar.

The size has been kept as one as it becomes out of bound on the first run for the first bar. A close examination would let you know that on the first bar, it is either pivot high or pivot low, and the loop condition discussed later becomes out of bound.

In case swh has a value, i.e. it is pivot high, the value of pivot high is stored at the top location of the array through the function array.unshift(). Similarly, for pivot low, the value of pivot low is stored in the array PL at line 27. Storing a new value of pivot increases the size of the array by 1.

```
29: for i=0 to array.size(PH)-1
30:    if close > array.get(PH,i)
31:       array.set(PH,i,10000)
32:       label1 = label.new(bar_index, low, text="", style=label.style_circle,size=size.tiny)
33:
34: for i=0 to array.size(PL)-1
35:    if close < array.get(PL,i)
36:       array.set(PL,i,0)
37:       label1 = label.new(bar_index, high, text="",color=color.red,
38:        style=label.style_circle,size=size.tiny)
```

Line no 29 is a loop fetching each element in the PH array. The loop range has been kept as array.size(PH)-1 because the array index starts from 0. Suppose you have five elements in the array, then the array size would be five, but the index would start from 0 to 4.

Line 30 checks the condition - whether the close is greater than the element's value in the array. The value of an element in the array is fetched through the function array.get(PH,i), where "i" is the index which starts from zero to the max index, i.e. array.size(PH)-1. This checks whether any element break out has occurred. In case of a breakout, lines 31 and 32 are executed, or the next element is compared.

In line 31, we have changed the value of the array to 10000 if a breakout has happened. This is done intentionally to mark the breakout element so that the element can be removed in subsequent codes. There are many other methods to remove an element; however, we have done this to demonstrate the use of functions to remove an element from the array.

In line no 32, the label function marks a solid circle below the bar. This is simple and has already been discussed.

Similarly, in lines 34 to 38, we have done the same for the PL array. However, we have changed the breakout value to zero.

```
40: if array.indexof(PH,10000) > 0
41:   array.remove(PH,array.indexof(PH,10000))
42:
43: if array.indexof(PL,0) > 0
44:   array.remove(PL,array.indexof(PL,0))
```

From line no 40 to line no 44, we have code to remove all the elements marked earlier. We have marked the pivot high as 10000, and the pivot low has been marked with zero. We have searched for the index of these values and have removed them using function array.remove().

Summary

- Arrays should be used when you require to store some value for future use.
- Arrays have many built-in functions for adding, removing, and doing mathematical operations.
- The maximum index of an array is one less than the size of the array.
- Arrays are created for all bars.
- The value of any array element is a series, not a single value.

Chapter 23: Swing high/low breakout strategy

In the previous chapters, we learned about pivot high/low indicators and a breakout strategy using the array. In this chapter, we will make a trading strategy around pivot high/low.

Below is the result of the strategy on a 3 min chart of SBIN (State Bank of India) from the NSE exchange for a period from 28th Feb 22 to 28th March 22, i.e. for a month.

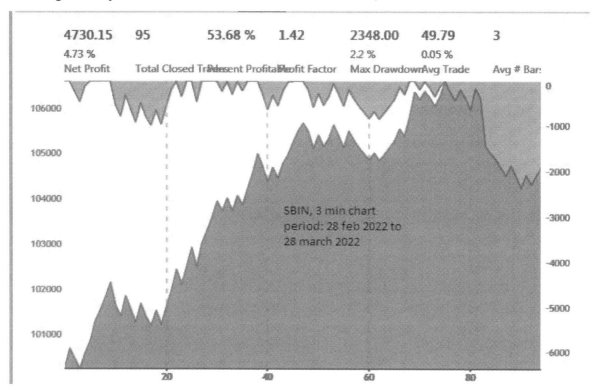

The script has taken 95 trades with a 53.68% success rate. Although the success rate is low, the script has made a profit of INR 49.79 on each trade with an initial capital of INR 100,000. If I deduct brokerage from the profit per trade, even then the trades are profitable. The buy and hold strategy during the period would have yielded 3.37%.

During the backtesting period, the price of the stock of SBIN had moved in both directions, making a deep "V" shape. The trend of the stock during the period is shown below:

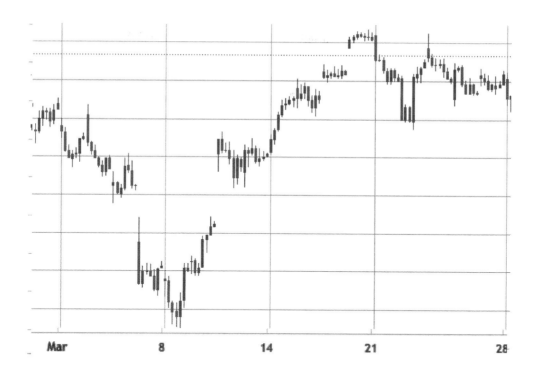

When the strategy is applied to APPLE on 3 min chart for the same period, the result of $100,000 initial capital for the same period is shown below :

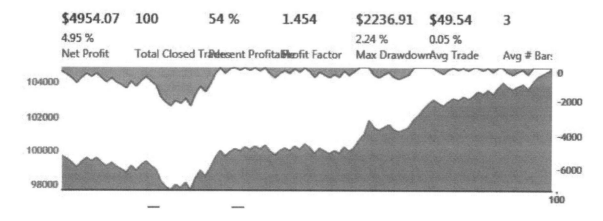

$4954.07	100	54 %	1.454	$2236.91	$49.54	3
4.95 %				2.24 %	0.05 %	
Net Profit	Total Closed Trades	Percent Profitable	Profit Factor	Max Drawdown	Avg Trade	Avg # Bars

Each trade resulted in a profit of $49.54. During the period under backtesting, the strategy took 100 trades.

The Strategy

The strategy used is simple, as soon as a bar breaks a recently formed pivot high, a long position can be taken and if the bar breaks the recently formed pivot low a short position can be considered. The swing point is identified using pivot indicator of pinescript. Further, the trading strategy is refined in the upcoming sections by using additional filters.

Coding the strategy

The major parts of the code are as under :

1. A time window for backtesting allowing a user to select the backtesting period. We have already done this in earlier codes.
2. Code for creating and marking pivot points
3. Code to identify breakout of a recent pivot point
4. Order placing
5. Exiting from trade
6. Refine Entry by filters

Coding time-window function

The first part of creating a time window for backtesting is given below. We have used this code several times in the past; therefore, I feel there is no need to explain this code.

```
//@version=5
strategy("Pivot Trade Strategy", overlay=true)

///-----------------------------date range-------------------------
// === INPUT BACKTEST RANGE ===
FromMonth = input.int(defval = 2, title = "From Month", minval = 1, maxval = 12)
FromDay   = input.int(defval = 28, title = "From Day", minval = 1, maxval = 31)
FromYear  = input.int(defval = 2022, title = "From Year", minval = 2015)
ToMonth   = input.int(defval = 3, title = "To Month", minval = 1, maxval = 12)
ToDay     = input.int(defval = 28, title = "To Day", minval = 1, maxval = 31)
ToYear    = input.int(defval = 2022, title = "To Year", minval = 2022)

// === FUNCTION EXAMPLE ===
start   = timestamp(FromYear, FromMonth, FromDay, 00, 00)  // backtest start window
finish  = timestamp(ToYear, ToMonth, ToDay, 23, 59)        // backtest finish window
window() => time >= start and time <= finish ? true : false // create function "within window of time"
//----------------------------------------------------------------
```

Coding and marking pivots

The pivot points can be calculated using pivothigh and pivotlow functions of the pine script. These are located inside the technical indicator library of pinescript; therefore, we have to use prefix "ta" before the name of these functions.

The pivothigh and pivotlow functions have also been discussed in this book. These functions can take three arguments. The first two are the numbers of left and right bars used for the calculation. The third argument is optional. In the case of pivothigh, the third argument is high by default, and for pivotlow, the third argument is low. Even if the third argument is not supplied, the function takes the default values and does the calculation.

```
///code for Recent Pivot Point///
leftBars  = input(4)
rightBars = input(2)

swh = ta.pivothigh(leftBars, rightBars)
swl = ta.pivotlow(leftBars, rightBars)

swh_cond = not na(swh)
swl_cond = not na(swl)

plotshape(swh_cond, text = "PH", color = color.green, style = shape.arrowdown, location =
location.abovebar, offset = -rightBars)
plotshape(swl_cond, text = "PL", color = color.red,   style = shape.arrowup,   location =
location.belowbar, offset = -rightBars)
//-----------------pivot drawing ended------------------------
```

The above code uses 4 and 2 numbers for left and right bars. The purpose of the function is to identify swing points. The function considers seven bars simultaneously with the default setting of 4 left and 2 right bars. If the bar under consideration is highest among 4 left and 2 right bars, the bar can be considered a high swing point. The function stores the value of the identified swing high otherwise, a NAN value is stored. The graphical representation of the concept for calculation of pivot high and pivot low points is shown below:

High	4	5	6	7	8	4	3	2
PH offset=2	Nan	Nan	Nan	Nan	8	Nan	Nan	Nan

The swing value is stored as soon as it is identified, but the swing value can only be identified after a lapse of at least 2 bars. Thus pivot point identification lags by 2 bars.

Similarly, for pivot low, the lowest value among the 4 left bars and 2 right bars are looked for; if the lowest value of a bar is the lowest among 4 left bars and 2 right bars, the lowest of the bar can be considered as pivot low.

In the above code, the value of pivot high is stored in a variable named "swh" and pivot low is stored in a variable "swl". Both these variables are series variables. In case the bar is a pivot, the variables "swh"/"swl" has a value equal to swing high or low as the case may be. Otherwise, "na" is stored as shown in the above chart.

Further, the code draws pivots on the chart using the plotshape function. An offset equivalent to "right bars" value is used in the plotshape. This is done as the pivots are lagging by two bars, and their identification only happens after two bars have lapsed.

Code to identify breakout of recent pivot point

Before the breakout of the recent pivot is coded, we need to know the value of the recent pivot point. The value of the recent pivot can be obtained through the below code:

```
//----------------find recent PH -----------
PH = ta.valuewhen(not na(swh),swh,0)

//----------------find recent PH -----------
PL = ta.valuewhen(not na(swl),swl,0)
```

The code stores the recent pivot high value in PH and the recent pivot low value in PL. If you have a problem understanding the above code, look at the explanation given below.

The pinescript has a function "valuewhen" in the technical analysis library of pinescript. The function takes three arguments.
1. The condition which when true the value is to be returned
2. The series from which value has to be returned
3. The number of occurrence. For a recent occurrence the value will be zero and for one before recent occurrence, the value will be 1 and so on.

Let's take a series variable named "myVariable" with the following values for each bar. In the example given below, the bar-index have index of the bar. Assume bar with the bar_index value of 1 is the recent bar:

bar_index	1	2	3	4	5	6	7	8	9
myVariable	5	76	8	9	3	56	7	8	99

Let's say we want to know the variable value when it is more than 10.

Code	Result
ta.valuewhen(myVariable>10,myVariable,0)	76
ta.valuewhen(myVariable>10,myVariable,1)	56
ta.valuewhen(myVariable>10,myVariable,2)	99

Now say I want to know the bar_index, when myVariable was more than 10.

Code	Result
ta.valuewhen(myVariable>10,bar_index,0)	2
ta.valuewhen(myVariable>10, bar_index,1)	6
ta.valuewhen(myVariable>10, bar_index,2)	9

Equipped with the above knowledge, code for identifying the event of a breakout of recent pivot high or pivot low value.

The breakout can be through a gap up or gap down. If we do not consider breakouts with gaps, a breakdown is when open of a bar is above the pivot low and close is below the pivot. And similarly, for breakout from above, the open value should be below the pivot high and close value should be above pivot high.

Considering the gap, the previous bar's close should be below the pivot high, and the current bar close above the pivot high. The condition gets reversed in the case of breakdown.

This condition can now be coded as :

```
//Buy Condition-------
//bar just crossed recent PH

go_long = 0
if(open <= PH and close >= PH or close[1] <= PH and close >=PH)
    go_long:=1

//short Condition-------
//bar just crossed recent PL
go_short = 0
if(open >= PL and close <= PL or close[1] >= PL and close <=PL)
    go_short:=1
```

Placing Order

Before placing order by using strategy.entry function , we need to calculate the units that we wish to buy with the available capital. For this, we can divide strategy.equity i.e. total initial fund plus profit and any unrealized profit with the close price of the equity. The number of is rounded down to the nearest integer by using the floor function from the math library of the pine script.

```
ordersize=math.floor(strategy.equity/(close))
strategy.entry("Long", strategy.long,ordersize,limit=close, when = window() and go_long)
strategy.entry("Short",  strategy.short,ordersize,limit=close,  when  =  window()  and
go_short)
```

The quantity of stock that we can buy with the available fund is now stored in the variable name ordersize. We invoke strategy.entry function to place order. The condition for going long or short is stored in the variable go_long and go_short. We add window() function to it so that order is between the backtesting period. The order is placed with a limit price of close. This can be disputed, you can also use pullback to the pivot point for placing order. Some can also argue that the price will move rapidly and placing an order on close may not fulfill.

I leave this upto you for decision. I am using limit order with close value for placing order.

Exiting from trade

Once we have taken a position, it is important to have an exit. The exit can be taken with fixed profit target or you can just trail your stop so that when price starts moving in an adverse direction , the position is exited.

```
strategy.exit("Exit long","Long", stop=strategy.position_avg_price - ta.atr(7),trail_points =
ta.atr(7)/syminfo.mintick, comment="Exit true")

strategy.exit("Exit Short","Short",stop=strategy.position_avg_price + ta.atr(7), trail_points =
ta.atr(7)/syminfo.mintick, comment="Exit true")
```

I have used profit target as atr(7) in the above code. The profit target is assigned to the parameter trail_points in tick points by dividing the absolute value of ATR with the minimum tick size defined by system variable syminfo.mintick.

The stop loss value is defined in price and assigned to the parameter stop. The stoploss in both the cases is kept atr(7) away from the entry price.

Now, we will add all the code snippets and run our strategy. The result generated by this strategy for APPL for one month from 28th Feb to 28th March 22 is as under :

$7280.58	248	45.97 %	1.023	$52391.47	$29.36	3
0.73 %				5.24 %	0 %	
Net Profit	Total Closed Trades	Percent Profitable	Profit Factor	Max Drawdown	Avg Trade	Avg # Bars

Refine Entry by filters

There is a need for improving entry. We can improve the entry by apply some filters. The first filter that comes to my mind is that in case of actual breakout or break down we must have some background for assuming breakout in that direction. This can be judged by the existing trend. If the existing trend is already bullish , we should not take a short and look for bullish opportunity. Trend as a filter can be used.

There could be various ways to look for trend. Some may take reference from EMA or SMA to establish trend. However, I am using another method for establishing trend.

I will count the number of green and red candles for last 14 periods and if the red candles are more, I will assume it as a bearish trend and if the green candles are more , I will assume it as a bullish trend.

The code for establishing trend by counting red and green candle is below:

```
//-----------trend finder----------------
sum = 0
X = for i = 1 to 14
    if(close[i]>open[i])
        sum :=sum +1
    if(close[i]<open[i])
        sum :=sum -1
//----------trend ended------------
```

Now if the value of the sum variable is positive, it is a bullish trend and if the value of the sum variable is negative, it is a bearish trend.

The trend can be incorporated in the strategy.entry function as under :

```
strategy.entry("Long", strategy.long,ordersize,limit=close, when = window() and go_long and sum > 0)

strategy.entry("Short", strategy.short,ordersize,limit=close, when = window() and go_short and sum < 0)
```

The result obtained from the above code for APPL is shown below:

$5508.15	155	50.32 %	1.324	$2311.74	$35.54	3
5.51 %				2.31 %	0.04 %	
Net Profit	Total Closed Trades	Percent Profitable	Profit Factor	Max Drawdown	Avg Trade	Avg # Bar:

Can this result be improved? Have a close look on the bars where losing positions have been taken by the system. You will notice that in some cases for a breakout on upside, the price have opened gap-up and then closed below the open. This should not be accepted.

Similarly for a breakdown on lowerside. The price have gap down and close is higher than the open. These cases may be excluded from the entry as these may be early signs of weakness in the trend and price may get reverse.

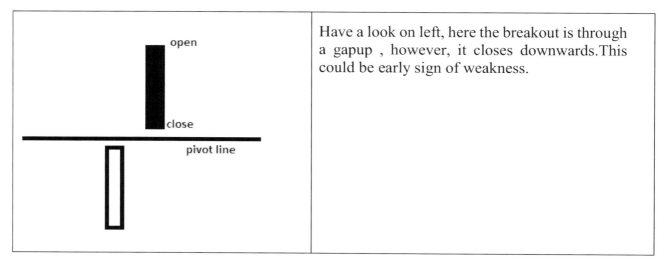

  open close pivot line	Have a look on left, here the breakout is through a gapup , however, it closes downwards.This could be early sign of weakness.

We can also use volatility as another measure for filtering out entry. We are since looking ATR(7) as our target price. We must have a strong move for breakout. The range of the bar must be atleast greater than the ATR value.

```
//-----Additional Buy Condition-------------------//
// volitility + green bar + up trend //
go_long1 = 0
if(((high-low)/ta.atr(7))>1 and open < close and sum > 1 )
    go_long1:= 1
//--------Condition ends-----


//-----Additional Short Condition-----------------//
//volitility + red bar + down trend
go_short1=0
if(((high-low)/ta.atr(7))>1 and open > close  and sum < -1)
    go_short1:=1
```

Now after incorporating the above code our entry condition will also change to the following:

```
strategy.entry("Long", strategy.long,ordersize,limit=close, when = window() and go_long and go_long1)
```

```
strategy.entry("Short", strategy.short,ordersize,limit=close, when = window() and go_short
and go_short1)
```

The result obtained after the above is as under :

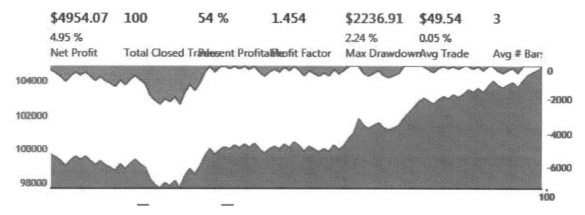

$4954.07	100	54 %	1.454	$2236.91	$49.54	3
4.95 %				2.24 %	0.05 %	
Net Profit	Total Closed Trades	Percent Profitable	Profit Factor	Max Drawdown	Avg Trade	Avg # Bars

This is an attempt to demonstrate the coding deatures of pinescript and ability of the
script to code trading strategies. You can use RSI , volume or any other additional
paranmeter for refining entry and exit.

The Complete Code

```
//@version=5
strategy("Pivot Trade Strategy", overlay=true)

///--------------------------------date range-------------------------
// === INPUT BACKTEST RANGE ===
FromMonth = input.int(defval = 2, title = "From Month", minval = 1, maxval = 12)
FromDay   = input.int(defval = 28, title = "From Day", minval = 1, maxval = 31)
FromYear  = input.int(defval = 2022, title = "From Year", minval = 2015)
ToMonth   = input.int(defval = 3, title = "To Month", minval = 1, maxval = 12)
ToDay     = input.int(defval = 28, title = "To Day", minval = 1, maxval = 31)
ToYear    = input.int(defval = 2022, title = "To Year", minval = 2022)

// === FUNCTION EXAMPLE ===
start   = timestamp(FromYear, FromMonth, FromDay, 00, 00) // backtest start window
finish  = timestamp(ToYear, ToMonth, ToDay, 23, 59)      // backtest finish window
window() => time >= start and time <= finish ? true : false // create function "within window of time"

//------------------------------------------------------------
///code for Recent Pivot Point///
leftBars  = input(4)
rightBars = input(2)
```

```
swh = ta.pivothigh(leftBars, rightBars)
swl = ta.pivotlow(leftBars, rightBars)

swh_cond = not na(swh)
swl_cond = not na(swl)

plotshape(swh_cond, text = "PH", color = color.green, style = shape.arrowdown, location = location.abovebar,
offset = -rightBars)
plotshape(swl_cond, text = "PL", color = color.red,   style = shape.arrowup,   location = location.belowbar, offset
= -rightBars)
//----------------pivot drawing ended------------------------

//----------------find recent PH -----------
PH = ta.valuewhen(not na(swh),swh,0)
//----------------find recent PL -----------
PL = ta.valuewhen(not na(swl),swl,0)

//-----------trend finder----------------
sum = 0
X = for i = 1 to 14
    if(close[i]>open[i])
        sum :=sum +1
    if(close[i]<open[i])
        sum :=sum -1
//----------trend ended------------

//-----Buy Condition1-------------------//
// volitility + green bar + up trend //
go_long = 0
if(((high-low)/ta.atr(7))>1 and open < close and sum > 1 )
    go_long:= 1
//--------Condition 1 ends-----

//-----Short Condition1-----------------//
//volitility + red bar + down trend
go_short=0
if(((high-low)/ta.atr(7))>1 and open > close  and sum < -1)
    go_short:=1

//Buy Condition2-------
//bar just crossed recent PH

go_long1 = 0
if(open <= PH and close >= PH or close[1] <= PH and close >=PH)
    go_long1:=1

//short Condition2-------
//bar just crossed recent PL
go_short1 = 0
if(open >= PL and close <= PL or close[1] >= PL and close <=PL)
    go_short1:=1
```

```
ordersize=math.floor(strategy.equity/(close))
strategy.entry("Long", strategy.long,ordersize,limit=close, when = window() and go_long and go_long1  )
strategy.entry("Short", strategy.short,ordersize,limit=close, when = window() and go_short and go_short1  )

strategy.exit("Exit long","Long", stop=strategy.position_avg_price - ta.atr(7),trail_points =
ta.atr(7)/syminfo.mintick,comment="Exit true")
strategy.exit("Exit Short","Short",stop=strategy.position_avg_price + ta.atr(7), trail_points =
ta.atr(7)/syminfo.mintick,comment="Exit true")
```

Chapter 24: Webhooks: Opportunity to trade outside TradingView.

The webhooks feature provided by alert in tradingview can be used to extract data or trade signals from tradingview to another platform for trading purposes. Till now we had only discussed backtesting, and indicator development in pinescript, but have not discussed using pinescript for live trading through a broker's external API.

You must be aware that tradingview supports brokers for live trading through tradingview charts, but does not allow pinescript strategies to place an order directly to broker. This limitation can be overcome by clubbing tradingview signals with the APIs provided by brokers to develop a functional automatic trading system. This trading system can use algo from tradingview or can track price movements using tradingview and place an order through your brokers through API provided by your broker.

What are webhooks?

A webhook can be considered an API (data sharing on a web server) that is triggered by an event. So let's say there is a buy signal generated on the tradingview platform, and then the webhook can transfer the trigger signal to another server.

The option to activate Webhook is under an alert window, as shown on the left.

Selecting the webhook feature allows you to provide the URL of your server where data from the trading view is to be transferred.

When an alert is triggered, webhook can be activated to transfer data from tradingview to the web server address defined by you. This means you have to run a webserver on your machine to receive the data.

The webhook feature is not available to free members of tradingview. Either you can have a trial of paid services to explore features or you can directly purchase a tradingview subscription for utilizing its paid services including the webhook feature.

Setting up Server to Receive Data

For receiving data through an alert webhook from tradingview you need to set up a server on your computer. This can be done in many ways. In this section, we will be using python's flask module to capture data from the webhook of tradingview.

I assume that you have basic knowledge of python. Python is outside the scope of this book. You may refer to my other book, "Teach Yourself Python Backtrader: Step by Step backtesting implementation for non-programmers". The book teaches the Backtrader module of python for implementing backtesting using python. In the book, python basics are also covered for non-programmers.

The below code requires that you install the flask module of python and execute this simple code.

```
from flask import Flask
app = Flask(__name__)

@app.route("/")
def fun_root():
    return "<p>Hello, World!</p>"
app.run()
```

For all those who are not aware of the functioning of a web server, this is for you people. Others may skip it. The address of the local machine where you are making your code has a local IP address which is 127.0.0.1. When an instance of the flask is executed, a server is created on this IP address at port no 5000. This web server should be regarded as a developmental web server as it can be created without administrator permission. All port numbers above 1024 do not require admin permission.

The default address of the root will be http://127.0.0.1:5000 and is denoted by ("/") i.e. root folder.

When the default web address is opened, the function fun_root() is executed returning the "Hello, World!" string on the web browser. What if, my web address is other than the above, for example, http://127.0.0.1:5000/about? This throws error.

You must find out the external IP number of the PC so that the server created in the last code can be connected. On the command prompt of windows use the "ipconfig" command to get the IP number of your PC.

```
C:\Users\achal>ipconfig

Windows IP Configuration

Wireless LAN adapter Wi-Fi:

    Connection-specific DNS Suffix   . :
    Link-local IPv6 Address . . . . . : fe80::1024:4359
    IPv4 Address. . . . . . . . . . . : 192.168.0.103
    Subnet Mask . . . . . . . . . . . : 255.255.255.0
    Default Gateway . . . . . . . . . : 192.168.0.1

C:\Users\achal>
```

The above IP number of my PC is 192.168.0.103 and is a local IP and can only be connected from any computer within the local area network. If a router is installed at home so from any computer at home using the above IP, the computer can be connected, but from the office or any computer outside the network cannot connect the PC.

So what is external IP? You can search for "my IP address" on google and the first result provides your IP address. In my case, the public IP address is 111.91.230.236. If anyone connects to this IP number with the port number (http:// 111.91.230.236:5000) in a browser through an external computer or network device like a phone, and have a "hello world" message displayed on the browser from the flask server, congratulation! you have made it.

Most probably you won't be able to connect to the flask server from any device external to the network, because in most cases computers are behind a firewall provided by a Service provider, router or your local computer's firewall is not allowing a connection.

To check whether IP is accessible from an external network, I connect my computer to a home network and try to browse public IP and port of the computer through a mobile connected to a mobile network which is different from the home network. I was not able to connect to the computer as the browser returned "page not found error". If successfully connected to the computer server, the result could have been "Hello World!".

A way around NAT/firewall

In case are behind a firewall or NAT, your computer may not be accessible directly from the internet. It means you can make an outgoing connection, but others cannot make an incoming connection to your computer. Generally, it means that you do not have a static IP, and the IP keeps on changing.

To make things simpler, let me explain the entire concept in simpler terms. All computers have IP addresses i.e. Internet Protocol addresses. But since the number of computers connected to the internet has increased, it is not possible to provide every computer with a unique IP number.

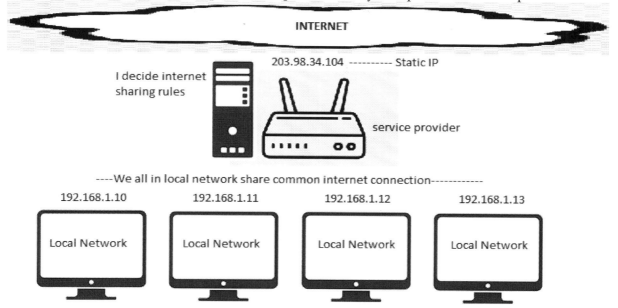

Generally, your service provider has an IP address connected to the internet, is recognized on the internet, and can send and receive data. The service provider uses routers and other types of hardware and distributes internet connection to other users in the locality. Now whatever you do, the data will flow in and out from the IP address of your service provider.

To enhance security, routers (the hardware with the service provider) generally do not allow incoming connections to pass through routers. You can receive incoming connection only if you make a configuration to the router but it is with the service provider. You can request the service provider or search for other ways to receive incoming connections.

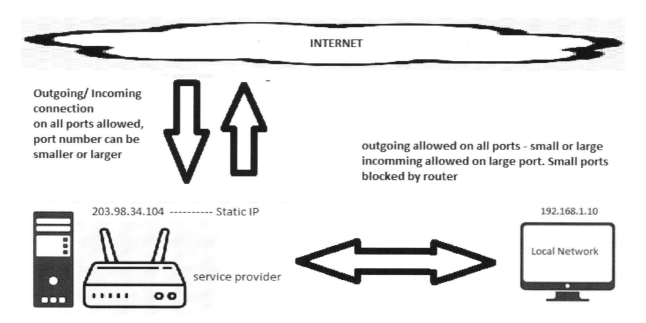

With a mobile, can you receive two simultaneous calls? Or can you dial two different people? A computer connected to the internet can simultaneously connect to different websites and applications on the internet. You can open a google search engine and at the same time can also check email and do chatting on the computer. That means your computer can simultaneously connect to one or more computers online. But, when an IP is connected to google and if the same IP gets connected to a chatting website, is there any chance of mixing data from one website with data from another website or chat? Can data from the website get delivered in chat?

All IP numbers while connecting to other computers use "ports". Using ports allows them to connect to multiple computers through a single IP. Using a "netstat" command on the command prompt gives details of all IP addresses connected with the PC along with their port :

```
Microsoft Windows [Version 10.0.17134.2208]
(c) 2018 Microsoft Corporation. All rights reserved.

C:\Users\achal>netstat -n

Active Connections

  Proto  Local Address          Foreign Address        State
  TCP    192.168.43.134:63406   78.47.204.111:443      ESTABLISHED
  TCP    192.168.43.134:63810   20.198.162.78:443      ESTABLISHED
  TCP    192.168.43.134:63922   117.18.237.29:80       CLOSE_WAIT
  TCP    192.168.43.134:63926   142.250.196.42:443     CLOSE_WAIT
```

Generally, any server can accept multiple connections by assigning one port per application. Accepting connection is not allowed by routers or firewalls and you can overcome this by use of any tunnelling software and turning off your firewall.

In this case, we want to accept "http" webhook connections from tradingview, we need to keep one port open for listening to webhook calls. In case a computer is not accessible from an outside network, I suggest downloading ngrok from the internet to allow the tunnelling to accept connection from tradingview.

Configuring NGROK

For using ngrok, search ngrok from google and download ngrok to your computer. Assuming you are a windows user, download the ngrok and extract the ngrok.exe file to a folder of your choice.

Now visit the website of ngrok and signup for a free account. Our work can be done with free signup and there is no need for purchase. Once signed in, on the dashboard, you have a link on the left navigation panel named "Your Authtoken". Click it and obtain your authtoken.

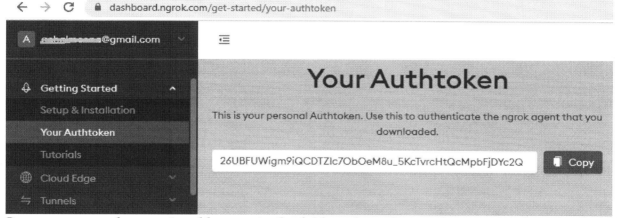

Open a command prompt and browse to the folder where the ngrok executive downloaded file is saved. Now issue the following command on the command prompt:

```
$ngrok authtoken your_auth_token_pasted_here
```

This command generates a configuration file in the folder where ngrok downloaded files are stored. If you want to open the computer's port 5000 to accept webhook calls, issue the following command

```
ngrok http 5000
```

The above command opens port 5000 on computer through tunnel allowing anyone to connect to port 5000 of the computer. You get a window like this:

```
ngrok by @inconshreveable

Session Status    online
Account           ac█████████@gmail.com (Plan: Free)
Version           2.3.40
Region            United States (us)
Web Interface     http://127.0.0.1:4040
Forwarding        http://6cff-111-91-230-202.ngrok.io -> http://localhost:80
Forwarding        https://6cff-111-91-230-202.ngrok.io -> http://localhost:80

Connections       ttl       opn       rt1       rt5       p50       p90
                  493       0         0.00      0.00      2.42      6.09

HTTP Requests
```

The web URL that connects to your computer's port 5000 is **http://6cff-111-91-230-202.ngrok.io**. You can use the URL generated by ngrok to connect to your computer from any external network. This can bypass all firewalls and routers. You can also use this URL in tradingview's webhook setting for a hassle-free connection to your computer. Ensure that the above ngrok window is kept open till you are receiving the data from tradingview.

Integrating with API of broker

Integration with the broker API for order placement and coding in python is not in the scope of this book. However, how alert signals can be received from a trading view is explained below.

For a simple moving average strategy for a buy-trigger create one alert and for a sell-signal create another alert. On the left is the buy-side alert.

The webhook URL for the server obtained from the ngrok is provided in the webhook URL field. Under the message, provide details of data that is needed to be sent from tradingview to the server when an alert condition is triggered.

The data to be sent should be in a JSON format i.e. under curly brackets in pairs separated by commas as shown below:
{"ticker":"ETH","side":"buy"}

Once the alert is triggered the JSON data is delivered to the flask server running on our computer.

The flask server code in python is given below:

```python
from flask import Flask, request
app = Flask(__name__)

@app.route("/")
def fun_root():
    if request.method == 'POST':
        print("Data received from Webhook is: ", request.json)
        alert = request.get_json()
        symbol = alert['ticker'] #symbol is stored in symbol variable
        side = alert['side'] # buy or sell side stored in the "side" variable.
    return "Webhook received"
app.run(host='0.0.0.0', port=8000)
```

As soon as a webhook alert is received through the 'POST' method, the function fun_root() is executed. The fun_root() first prints "Data received from Webhook is: {"ticker":"ETH","side":"buy"}" in the python console window, if the trigger was for the buy side. The request.get_json() on the next line obtains key-pair data and saves them in the "alert" variable. Each key-pair data can be accessed using the variable's name followed by the key name inside a square bracket as shown below:

```python
alert['side'] # it has value "buy"
```

Follow your broker's API for the order placement on the broker's server.

The above is the easiest way to take advantage of the pinescript strategy by the placement of live orders on your favourite broker. The latency time, i.e. time to travel data from the tradingview to your server, is generally low. In my case, it is around 120-200ms. Further, depending on your broker, order placement time could be anywhere between 20ms to 300ms. For all practical purposes, an order can be placed on your broker's server within 140ms to 500ms of alert generation on tradingview.

Appendix A – Answers to quizzes and exercises

Chapter -2

Q.1 True and False

B. Can a PineScript compiler see the comments within your Pine program? **- NO**

C. The value of close 4 bar back can be accessed using close[4]. **- YES**

D. The errors generated while executing the script are displayed in the debugging window. **- YES**

Q.2 Consider fig 2.4; what would be the value of close[0]? **– 36.4**

Q.3 Consider fig 2.4. what would be the value of close[1.5]? **– ERROR, not possible; only integer values are allowed**

Exercises

4. Modify the program shown in this lesson to plot a simple moving average of 14 periods on the chart.

```
1: // This source code is subject to the terms of the Mozilla Public License 2.0
2: // © Creating trade Strategies & Backtesting Using PineScript - UDEMY
3:
4: //@version=5
5: indicator("Plotting sma", overlay=true)
6: mySMA = ta.sma(close, 14)
7: plot(mySMA)
```

Chapter -3

4. Is this correct: plot(myEMA7,title="EMA7",color=color.red,linewidth=2.5) **– no linewidth cannot be float**

5. Is this code correct: plot(myEMA7,Title="EMA7",color=color.red,linewidth=2) **– "T" of title cannot be uppercase.**

6. Is this code correct: plot(myEMA7,"EMA7",color.red,linewidth=2) **- Yes**

Exercise

3. Write a script to plot sma of 3,7 and 14 period wherein the colour of all three lines should be different. 14-period sma should be most thick, followed by 7 and 3 periods.

```
1: // This source code is subject to the terms of the Mozilla Public License 2.0
2: // © Creating trade Strategies & Backtesting Using PineScript - UDEMY
3:
4: //@version=5
5: indicator("3 SMA plot", overlay=true)
6: mySMA3 = ta.sma(close,3)
7: mySMA7 = ta.sma(close,7)
8: mySMA14 = ta.sma(close,14)
9: plot(mySMA3,,color=color.green)
10: Plot(mySMA7,color=color.red)
11: plot(mySMA14,color=color.yellow)
```

4 – try yourself.

Chapter 4

Q1. The data type of HL2 inbuilt variable is: **4. Float Series**

Q2. If X = close[1.6] instruction is given, what would be stored in X: **4. Error**

Q3. Suppose X = 1.1 and Y = 2; if Y:=X instruction is given, Y would be : **4. 1.1**

Q4. You want to store information on the number of guests who dined at the Restaurant in the last 30 days. What datatype you should use: **4. Integer series**

Exercise Q1. You want to store details of rainfall per day in your city for 365 days. You would be required to calculate the average rainfall for 365 days. What datatype variable would you use to store rainfall? **- Float Series**

Chapter – 5

Q.1 In the statement PI = 3.14, what is the datatype of PI? - **float**

Q.2 Consider the following statements:

```
PI = 3.14
X = 4
Result = X > PI and X < 10
```

What would be the value of the Result? **- TRUE**

Q.3 Consider the following statements

```
PI = 3.14
X = 4
Result = X > PI or X > 10
```

What would be the value of the Result? - **TRUE**

Q.4 What would be 13 % 12? **The answer is 1, % would provide a reminder after division.**

Q.5 **Crossover of SMA by price**

Exercise

Q.1 In the statement

```
PI = 3.14
result = PI => 4
```

What would be the result after correcting the error? Why has this error appeared? **The error is because of improper use of the sign "=>" should be written as ">=".**

Q.2 Improve doji pinescript code by including EMA 50. If the close of doji is above EMA 50, put a red down triangle above the bar. If the close of doji is below EMA 50, put a green triangle below the bar.

Replace line 12 of the original code with these two lines of code:

```
plotshape(Is_OC_Equal and close > ta.ema(close,50), color = color.red, style = shape.triangledown, location =
location.abovebar, transp = 0)
plotshape(Is_OC_Equal and close < ta.ema(close,50), color = color.green, style = shape.triangleup, location =
location.belowbar, transp = 0)
```

Q3 Do it yourself

Chapter – 6

Q1. Answer = **6**

Q2. **Answer = 18**

Q3. Answer =   **error**

Exercise

Q1. Write a program to calculate the average volume for the last 14 periods. Plot it below chart.

```
1: // This source code is subject to the terms of the Mozilla Public License 2.0
2: // © Creating trade Strategies & Backtesting Using PineScript - UDEMY
3: //@version=5
4:indicator("Average volume using loop",overlay = false)
5: sum = 0.0
6: for counter = 0 to 13
```

```
7:    sum:= sum + volume[counter]
8: volume7 = sum/14
9: plot(volume7,color=color.yellow)
```

Chapter 7

Quiz

Q1. Answer =2

Q.2 Answer =2

Q.3 Answer = 300

Exercise

Q.1 Write IN.8 script using the "iff" statement only.

```
01: // © Creating trade Strategies & Backtesting Using PineScript - UDEMY
02: //@version=5
03: indicator("Nested iff statements",overlay = true)
04: color_value = color.blue
05: myplot = ta.sma(hl2,7)
06:  color_value = iff(rsi(close,7) < 30,color.red,iff(rsi(close,7>80,color.green,color.yellow)
07: plot(myplot,color=color_value,linewidth=3)
```

Q.2 Write IN.7 "Dynamic colouring of plot" using conditional operator statement (?).

```
1: // This source code is subject to the terms of the Mozilla Public License 2.0
2: // © Creating trade Strategies & Backtesting Using PineScript - UDEMY
3: //@version=5
4:indicator("IN.7 Dynamic coloring of plot",overlay = true)
5: color_const = close > open? color.green, color.red
6: plot((high+low)/2,color=color_const)
```

Chapter – 8

Quiz

Q1. What would be the value of myResult after execution of the following code, if ta.sma(close,7) is greater than ta.sma(close,14):

```
myResult = ta.sma(close,7) > ta.sma(close,14)? true: false
```

Answer : TRUE

Q2. What would be the value of myResult after execution of the following code, if ta.sma(close,7) is greater than ta.sma(close,14):

```
myCrossover() => ta.sma(close,7) > ta.sma(close,14)? true: false
myResult = myCrossover()
```

Answer : TRUE

Q3. What would be the value of myResult after execution of the following code, if ta.sma(close,7) is greater than ta.sma(close,14):

```
myCrossover() =>
        If (ta.sma(close,7) > ta.sma(close,14))
                myReturn =  true
        Else
                myReturn = false
        myReturn
```

```
myResult = myCrossover()
```
Answer : TRUE

Q4. What would be the value of myResult after execution of the following code, if myRSI value is 21

```
Crossing = true
myRSI = rsi(close, 14)
myBuy(Crossover,myRSI)=>
        If (Crossover == false)
                myDecision = false
        else if (myrsi < 25)
                myDecision = true
        myDecision
myResult = myBuy(Crossing,myRSI)
```
Answer: TRUE

Exercise

Q1. Write a function for finding the lowest of three numbers. Input would be three variables, and output should be the lowest of the three variables.

```
threeLowest(val1,val2,val3)=>
        _result = 99999999
        if(val1 < val2)
                if(val1 < val3)
                        _result = val1
                else
                        _result = val3
        else if(val2<val3)
                        _result = val2
                else
                        _result = val3
        _result
```

Chapter -9

Q1. Study the below code:

```
a= 1
b= 2
b= a+b
```
What is the error, and how can it be solved? **b variable is a mutable variable, and therefore:= should have been used b:= a+b**

Q2. Consider the following code:

```
myFun(a, b, c)=>
        Z = a+b -c
        Z
X = 2
Y = 3
Z = 9
T = myFun(X,Y,Z)
```

What would be the value of T? **-3**

Q3. Suppose a variable series "myVar" is represented visually as under:

5	7	na	9	6	na	0	3	2	1

How can you replace all 'na' with zeros?

By using the nz function

example nz(myVar)

Chapter -10
Quiz

Q1. What if the xloc value is not defined in the line function? What is the default value for the xloc function? **xloc.Bar_index**

Q2. What is the default value of the "extend" argument in a line function? **extend.none**

Q3.What are the compulsory arguments of line function? **X1, X2, Y1, Y2**

Exercise

Q. Is zigzag function calculation in the previous lesson and pivot high and pivot low with rightBar =1 and leftBar= 1 give the same result?

Draw yourself and compare

Chapter -11

Q1. Study the below code of line

      src = input(defval= 5,title="Take Profit")

      would the above code allow a user to input a value of 6.6? **yes, as the type is not set**

Q2. Change the above code to have integers from 2 to 8.

src = input(defval= 5,title="Take Profit",type=input.ingeter, minval=2,maxval=8)

Q3. For the code

      f = input(title="Level", type=XXXX, defval=5, minval=0, maxval=10, step=0.02)

      What would be the value of type?

Make it float to have a step as small as 0.02, type = input.float

Exercise Q1.: DO it YourSelf

INDEX

Made in United States
Orlando, FL
27 December 2024

56566542R00128